ERSKINE H. CHILDERS
PRESIDENT OF IRELAND
A BIOGRAPHY

ERSKINE H. CHILDERS
President of Ireland
a biography

John N. Young

With a foreword by Jack Lynch

COLIN SMYTHE
Gerrards Cross 1985

Copyright © 1985 by John Nichols Young

First published in 1985 by Colin Smythe Limited
Gerrards Cross, Buckinghamshire

British Library Cataloguing in Publication Data
Young, John Nichols
    Erskine H. Childers, President of Ireland
    1. Childers, Erskine, 1905–1974
    2. Ireland—Presidents—Biography
    I. Title
    941.7082′092′4   DA965.C4/

    ISBN 0-86140-195-6

Produced in Great Britain
Set by Action Typesetting of Gloucester
and printed and bound by
Billing & Sons Limited, Worcester

CONTENTS

ILLUSTRATIONS

Erskine H. Childers, President of Ireland, 1974
Three childhood photographs
The *Daily Sketch* front page, 25 November 1922
With his father and brother at Worthing, c.1919
On holiday in France, c.1928
A family portrait c.1942
The 1951 Fianna Fail Cabinet
Erskine Childers and Miss Rita Dudley, on the occasion
    of their marriage, 1952
The 1959 Fianna Fail Cabinet
Two *Dublin Opinion* cartoons, 1957 and 1959
With Mr. Brian Faulkner, 1967
At the Irish Embassy in London, May 1970
With the Taoiseach, Mr. Jack Lynch, 1973
With the winner of an anti-smoking poster campaign,
    January 1971
The inauguration ceremony of the fourth President of
    Ireland, 1973
With Lord Mountbatten, and receiving the Freedom of
    Sligo, August 1974
A sixty-eighth birthday family portrait
The state visit to Belgium
With the French Prime Minister, M. Jacques Chirac
Mrs. Childers laying a wreath on the President's grave

FOREWORD

JACK LYNCH
Taoiseach 1966–73, 1977–79

The keen analytic mind of Erskine Childers seemed to engross him at the most unexpected times. One could have had a meal with him in the dining-room of Leinster House with most affable and enjoyable conversation. A short time later he would pass one in the various corridors of the House, barely recognising one, if at all: such was his commitment to, and concentration on, the problems of whatever ministry he occupied at the time. This characteristic did not always endear him to his parliamentary colleagues, although they always understood and admired his total commitment to his brief.

It was always believed that Eamon de Valera had a special interest in the young Erskine Childers following the execution of his father, a close colleague of Dev during the Civil War. But this was not the reason for Erskine's appointment in the early 1940s as a junior minister in the Department of Local Government, his first step on the ladder of ministerial responsibility. Dev knew administrative talent when he saw it.

Erskine Childers's handling of subsequent ministerial portfolios completely justified de Valera's initial confidence in him. In his first full ministry — Posts and Telegraphs — he was outstandingly successful and innovative. As Minister for Health he fundamentally changed and co-ordinated the health services, and when he was responsible for the Department of Transport and Power the same pioneering qualities were displayed. For example, he appointed as permanent head of that department the first ever woman to occupy such a post in Ireland. This woman, Thekla Beere, well merited this appointment on her own qualifications and experience.

Erskine Childers and James Dillon, one-time leader of the Opposition, and before that Minister for Agriculture, were the best orators in the Irish Parliament during the period of my membership, which covered three full decades. Paradoxically, during Question Time in the Dáil Erskine often appeared to be ill-at-ease when supplementary questions were being thrown at him from all sides. I used to sit beside him, being next in seniority in the government, so I had a good opportunity of observing him. When the answers came, however, no matter how irrelevant the questions, he phrased them in impeccable sequence.

Then came the metamorphosis in Erskine Childers, the 'public' man. Victory in the Presidential election was by no means assured. But the sincerity of his thoughts about the role of the President and the future of the youth of the country in a caring and prosperous Ireland, the manner in which he expressed these thoughts during the election campaign allied to the dedicated work of the party organisation in the constituencies, brought him an outstanding victory.

How he endeared himself to all the people, young and old, during the short period of his outstanding Presidency will always be a matter for historical record.

INTRODUCTION
AND ACKNOWLEDGEMENTS

It was, perhaps, inevitable that with a deep and abiding affection for both islands I should be drawn to the fascinating and complementary careers of two essentially English gentlemen who dedicated themselves to the Nationalist politics of Ireland with diametrically opposite results. The name of Erskine Childers evokes varied and piquant memories of a father and son whose lives together form one of the most moving and unusual stories of the twentieth century.

The elder Erskine found fame and success in England as an author, scholar and amateur yachtsman before moving to Ireland in middle age to play a central part in events leading to the establishment of the modern Irish state. Misunderstood and maligned as few men in recent history, Childers senior was executed by order of the Free State Government in one of the most horrific episodes of the Civil War. At the time the death of an able and gifted man appeared to many as a futile waste, yet it proved to be only the end of a beginning.

The younger Erskine, then a sixteen-year-old public schoolboy, was permitted to make one short visit to his father in the death cell. During the final emotional moments together he promised to enter Irish politics and do everything possible to ensure that his father's name became a healing memory. This promise was the inspiration behind a life devoted to the cause of reconciliation between Irishmen and between Ireland and Britain. The path was far from easy but despite a background markedly different from his political colleagues he achieved high office and filled several Government posts with distinction, bringing ability, efficiency and an unusual objectivity to his work. When a further wave of trouble engulfed Ireland from the late 'sixties onwards, Erskine Childers's career reached its zenith as Tánaiste (Deputy Prime Minister) and subsequently President, his name being synonymous with peace after he had calmed the nation during the 1970 Arms Crisis.

Inevitably, biographies of the elder Erskine leave the reader in a bleak Dublin barrack square in 1922. When I suggested to President Childers's widow, Rita Childers, that the story should be taken forward half a century to finish more appropriately in the glory of St Patrick's Cathedral, with Monarchs and Rulers assembled to pay tribute to a loved and respected Head of State, she responded sympathetically. Her encouragement and help ever since have been invaluable and I acknowledge also generous hospitality and great kindness.

Other members of the family have given ready assistance and I am particularly grateful to the late President's elder son, Mr Erskine B. Childers, and to Mrs Emily Dow Eddy.

A large amount of correspondence between Mr Childers and his parents and his first wife, Ruth, is still extant and, together with the memories of friends and contemporaries, has provided a comprehensive and vivid picture of his early life at school and university in England when virtually overnight he had to reject some of the inbred values and loyalties of his early childhood. This and the subsequent struggle for identity and recognition while a hard-up young man with a wife and family to keep are matters to which he hardly ever alluded and will surprise some readers who associated him with an entirely privileged English background. To Sir Richard Acland, Bart., the Rev. Humphrey Whistler, C.R., the Hon. Mervyn Roberts and Mr J. B. Hope-Simpson I am especially indebted for recollections of incidents which took place well over sixty years ago.

Rather less personal material related to later years but the testimony of erstwhile Government colleagues and Civil

Servants has been vital in bridging gaps and attempting a broad assessment of Mr Childers's achievements. The former Taoiseach, Mr Jack Lynch, the former Prime Minister of Northern Ireland, the Rt. Hon. Lord O'Neill of the Maine, Mr Desmond O'Malley, T.D., Senator Eoin Ryan, S.C., Dr Thekla Beere, Dr Leon O'Broin and Mr Dermot Foley were all kind enough to see me and gave generously of their time. The late Lord Glenavy, the Rt. Rev. Bishop A. W. Heavener, Mrs Agnes Leslie-Craig, Mrs Lily O'Hagan, Mr Charles Acton, Mr James M. Dillon, Mr Oliver J. Flanagan, K.S.G., T.D., Mr N. McMahon, Mr Gilbert McCool, the late Mr Paul MacWeeney, Mr James Leonard, T.D., Mr Lorcan O'Neill, Mr R. G. Patton, Mr Charles Roberts and Mr C. E. F. Trench have all added invaluable information and recollections.

Mr William O'Sullivan and Mr Bernard Meehan at the Manuscript Library in Trinity College, Dublin, were always extremely helpful on my many visits and the erudite humour of the former was an added bonus. Mr Trevor Kaye at Trinity College, Cambridge, Miss Joyce C. Dauley at Wellesley College, Massachusetts, and Miss Joan Barry at the Confederation of Irish Industry are other Librarians to whom I am indebted. The staff at the National Library of Ireland were always willing to assist with a variety of queries.

My warm thanks are due to Mr Fintan Keogh, Mr John McEntee and Mr Seán Magee for much help and encouragement and to Mr Colin Smythe for sage advice on numerous matters. My daughter Sarah cheerfully produced a legible manuscript from disjointed scribble and I am indeed grateful to her. Any omissions and shortcomings are, of course, entirely my responsibility.

March 1984   John N. Young.

Chapter I
A LONDON CHILDHOOD

A few weeks before his untimely death in November 1974 President Erskine Hamilton Childers of Ireland received a party of members of the Ancient and Honorable Artillery Company of Massachusetts. Since visits by delegations from transatlantic organisations to the Presidential residence in Dublin's Phoenix Park were an everyday occurrence no especial comment was evoked but the occasion had peculiar significance for the President himself, turning his thoughts back to his parents and their profound and lasting influence over his own life.

Seventy-one years previously his parents had met during a visit by the Honourable Artillery Company of London to its sister unit in Boston, notable in being the first time since independence that British troops paraded on American soil. Robert Erskine Childers, a clerk in the House of Commons and author of two books about the exclusive part-time City Regiment with which he had served in the South African War, became acquainted with Miss Mary Alden Osgood, daughter of a physician practising in the fashionable Beacon Hill district of Boston. The handsome English soldier and the beautiful and talented American lady fell in love at first sight. After a whirlwind courtship their marriage, described by the President as made in Heaven, took place at Holy Trinity Church in Boston on 4 January 1904.

The Childers family can trace its ancestry back to the reign of King Edward III, the name deriving from the old English 'cildra hus' meaning children's house. From the end of the sixteenth century the seat was established in

South Yorkshire, initially at Carr House near Doncaster and later at Cantley Hall two miles away towards the Lincolnshire border. Following the marriage in 1797 of Colonel John Walbanke Childers, officer commanding the 11th Light Dragoons, to the Hon. Selina Eardley, considerable wealth was injected into the family as the bride was a grand-daughter of Sampson Gideon who founded the London Stock Exchange and became financial adviser to Sir Robert Walpole, the first British Prime Minister.

Several descendants of John and Selina Childers gained prominence. Their eldest son, John, was a Liberal M.P. for nearly twenty years, representing Cambridgeshire and later the Malton Division of Yorkshire. A grandson, Hugh Culling Eardley Childers, played a distinguished part in British politics between 1860 and 1892, holding high office in several of Gladstone's administrations. As First Lord of the Admiralty he determined to make the British fleet the equal of any two other maritime powers and as Secretary for War he instigated many reforms in the face of stiff opposition from the Prince of Wales and the Duke of Cambridge. A convinced Irish Home Ruler, he was a prominent supporter of the first Home Rule Bill in 1886 and at the time of his death in 1896 was Chairman of a Government Committee investigating financial relations between Ireland and Britain. He is buried at Cantley, Yorkshire, where St Wilfrid's Church contains many memorials to members of the Childers family.

Robert Caesar Childers, another grandson of John and Selina, was the grandfather of the Irish President. Born at Cantley in 1838 he joined the Ceylon Civil Service in 1860 and became secretary to the Governor. Attracted towards the various Singhalese dialects he was soon devoting much spare time to learning Pali. Indifferent health led to a premature return home and on the first day of 1867 he married Anna Barton of Glendalough at Laragh in County Wicklow, thus giving the family an Irish dimension. The Bartons had settled in Ireland about 1600 with various branches upholding the Ascendency tradition ever since in Fermanagh, Tipperary, Kildare and elsewhere.

Robert and Anna Childers settled in London and their five children were born there. The second son, Robert Erskine, the father of our subject, came into the world on 25 June 1870 at 58 Mount Street, Mayfair, but fate decreed that he would hardly know his parents. For Robert Caesar Childers died in 1876, by which time he was an Oriental scholar of international repute. His Pali Dictionary unveiled the rich store of Buddhist literature to the West and from 1872 he had been a Professor at University College, London. Anna only outlived him for a few years, by which time further inter-marriage between the Childers and Barton families meant that the orphaned children were brought up by their aunt and uncle in County Wicklow.

From an early age Robert Erskine Childers thus knew and loved Ireland. Throughout his years at Haileybury School and Trinity College, Cambridge he returned to spend holidays with his brother, sisters and Barton cousins, of whom Robert, the eldest, became his close friend and confidant. In Wicklow he relaxed, walked the hills and grew to know people from all walks of life. At Cambridge he dropped his first Christian name and acquired a reputation for debate, being a keen participant at the Union and Magpie and Stump Societies. Passing the Civil Service Examination with distinction he became a clerk in the House of Commons in 1895. He worked hard and played hard, spending many week-ends and the long Parliamentary vacations sailing his 7-ton yacht *Vixen* off the east coast of England and northwards as far as the Baltic. Ever eager for adventure he joined the Honourable Artillery Company as a horse-driver at the start of the Boer War, serving with the City Imperial Volunteers for about a year. When his diary of day-by-day experiences was published in 1901 it was the first major account of army life in the ranks, giving evidence of Childers's literary talent. This found wider expression two years later when his novel *The Riddle of the Sands* appeared, to be acclaimed then and ever

3

since as one of the finest yachting adventure stories to be written. The fact that it was written deliberately to warn England of the possibility of invasion by Germany has not reduced its appeal to later generations.

When, at the age of thirty-three, he accompanied the H.A.C. on its historic tour of America, Childers could look back on a decade crammed with activity and achievement since he left Cambridge. Still very much an 'establishment' man he was not quite the high Tory of pre-Boer War days, having experienced at close quarters the company of men from vastly different backgrounds to his own. So far as Ireland was concerned he recognised the merit of a degree of autonomy but believed that the interests of his mother's country were largely identical to those of his father's native land.

Courage and fortitude summed up the life of Mary Alden Osgood, known always as Molly to her family. After a serious accident in her third year she spent most of her childhood lying on a frame and was able to move only her head and hands. Virtually self-educated she owed much to a kindly librarian at Beacon Street Public Library in Boston who encouraged an interest in books and scholarship. Though her parents, Hamilton and Margaret Osgood, were of Protestant Anglo-Saxon descent they had friends in all strata of Massachusetts society. Among them was John Boyle O'Reilly, leader of the Boston Irish community in the 1880s. From him Molly learned of the famine years in Ireland and of aspects of British repression, for O'Reilly was a Fenian who had been deported to Australia in 1867 after spending time in English prisons.

Boston society turned out in force for the Childers – Osgood wedding, a persistent reverence for British blood ensuring that Molly was the envy of some of her friends. An Italian honeymoon was followed by a return to London in good time for the start of the new Parliamentary session in spring 1904. Probability of late or all-night sittings at the House of Commons necessitated residence within reasonable proximity to Westminster and the couple took a flat in a quiet crescent of mansion blocks just off Chelsea Embankment. Edwardian Chelsea retained an aura of Carlyle, Whistler and Wilde, yet the famous rubbed shoulders easily with humbler folk. Before long Erskine and Molly Childers were happily absorbed in London life and soon came a hint of even greater joy as Erskine revealed in a letter to his sisters who were touring India:

We are both writing to tell you of the wonderful hope that is rising in us. The excitement grows every day as the symptoms which could destroy it never come. Of course one cannot be positive medically speaking, yet awhile, but I myself have what is almost a conviction. Sweet little Molly blossoms and vibrates under it and indeed I think something wonderful should come of our union for it is perfect love. [1]

The seal was set on their happiness when Molly gave birth to a son at home, 13 Embankment Gardens, on 11 December 1905. Her husband was present at the birth, sharing, as he always endeavoured to, the joy or sadness of every experience with his wife. Named Erskine after his father (himself so named after the famous Lord Chancellor who was an ancestor on the Barton side) and Hamilton after his maternal grandfather, the infant brought enormous pleasure to his parents. Even so his father, in his wildest dreams, cannot have envisaged the full significance when he wrote sometime afterwards to Molly of their 'legacy to the world'.

Mild pleasure of a different kind came later in December 1905 when a Liberal Government was returned at the general election by a majority of landslide proportions. Those working at the Commons, the centre of the national stage, had seen the Conservatives under Balfour growing tired and the prospect of a fresh and talented reforming administration seemed more in keeping with the new hope being engendered by the Monarch. The spirit of Edwardian optimism promised that things really were about to change for the better. Materially the Childers family wanted for little and if they had Molly's parents would have provided. Perhaps the most cherished of their possessions never came to London, let alone Chelsea Embankment. *Asgard,* a 28-ton gaff ketch specially designed and built in Norway on the lines of Nansen's *Fram,* was a wedding-present from the Osgoods and spent most of the time moored on Southampton Water. In the first decade of the century yachting was essentially a preserve of the privileged.

At home the elder Erskine spent much time writing. Basil Williams, his erstwhile Westminster colleague and Boer War companion, has left a description of the large room at the flat and of his friend working away at the table quite oblivious to Erskine junior playing on the floor and other distractions. Between 1905 and 1910 Volume V of the *Times History of the South African War* and two other works on the art of warfare were penned as well as numerous articles. Literary figures were prominent among the wide circle they entertained. The opinions of Erskine senior and Molly, whose broad culture and span of knowledge soon impressed her husband's English friends, were increasingly sought on a variety of subjects.

Young Erskine Childers's childhood was fairly typical for the scion of an upper-class London family of the period, comfortable, secure and stable. His baby years were spent largely in the care of 'Flodgy', the trusted nanny, who became an almost indispensable part of the domestic scene. Her physical disability made Molly unable to lift or carry her son, yet from the beginning an exceptionally close emotional bond existed between them and the boy's every development was watched with pride and fascination by both parents. In his perambulator baby Erskine was taken to near-by Ranelagh Gardens, along Chelsea Embankment or further afield to Battersea Park.

It was difficult to imagine that the throbbing heart of the metropolis was less than a mile away from Embankment Gardens, for there was an open aspect from the front across the River Thames and to the rear over the grounds of the Royal Hospital, home of the Chelsea Pensioners. Today the incessant roar of heavy traffic along the Embankment causes concern and disturbance but as Erskine lay in bed listening for his father to return home from the House of Commons few sounds broke the quietness outside. A horse-drawn carriage turning in the crescent, an occasional greeting from a passing tug on the river and the distant noise of trains on the approaches to Victoria Station could be heard intermittently but little else.

On the south bank of Chelsea Reach lay the broad acres of Battersea Park where London's two worlds came together and sometimes clashed. Youngsters from Chelsea and Pimlico on the north side, usually under the watchful eyes of nannies, shared the facilities with urchins from the less salubrious Clapham and Battersea in the south. Erskine was taken here regularly and as soon as he could comprehend was taught to observe and appreciate the wonders of nature through the changing seasons. Here also, as he grew older, he enjoyed imaginary adventures with his father, who would hire a boat on the lake and pretend to his son that they were shipwrecked and escaping from savages. Once he was old enough he ventured across on his own to play cricket or 'footer' and sometimes returned home muddied yet fulfilled. The earliest surviving letter from father to son was written on his fifth birthday in December 1910 and the carefully printed sentences give an early indication of what was expected from him:

You are five years old now and a big boy. Soon you will be a man. Be manly and truthful and loving. Take care of your darling mother who takes care of you and loves you so. Be unselfish and tender to everybody.

A few weeks later, just before his brother Robert was born, Erskine commenced his formal education at a small private kindergarten school run by a Mrs Spencer in Anhalt Road on the Battersea side of the Thames, just south of Albert Bridge. His classmates included Richard Acland, whose father, Sir Francis, was Liberal M.P. for

North West Cornwall and a junior minister in the Asquith Government. Acland became leader of 'Royal Richard's Pirate Corps', a group of the most adventurous boys at the school, whose antics included hanging on to the backs of horse-drawn vehicles, scavenging on the Thames mud flats and throwing dried horse dung at the music mistress! However, Erskine shunned involvement in the 'piratical' activities and was regarded as rather cleverer than most of the other pupils. His supreme interest at the time was electricity and he could be a positive bore on the subject. Passing one day the large clock which used to stand on Chelsea Embankment, Erskine asked Acland how he thought it worked. The latter, now Sir Richard, recalls playing dim by suggesting clockwork, steam, gas and so on in order to give his friend the pleasure of uttering his great word.

In the years between 1910 and the outbreak of war in 1914 father and son saw more of each other than at any other time. Prompted by Molly, who believed his ability to be worthy of greater things, the elder Erskine resigned his clerkship in Parliament with a view to becoming a Liberal Parliamentary candidate to fight for the causes nearest his heart. His conversion to a constitutional Irish Home Ruler had been completed by observations made in the rural west during a motor tour with Robert Barton in 1908, and this was the first of several major decisions which were to have a profound effect on his own life and the lives of his wife and sons. Alas, political ambition seemed doomed to frustration and failure. Eventual adoption as prospective candidate for the Devonport Division involved numerous journeys to Plymouth but ended after seventeen months in resignation and disappointment. His major contribution to contemporary politics was through the written word, usually on the subject of Ireland: an essay on the Land question for the Liberal Home Rule group, innumerable letters to *The Times* and his tome *The Framework of Home Rule*, widely regarded then and since as the classic statement of the case.

In between absences in Ireland or Devon, Childers senior

was often at home, able to break off from his work to take Erskine out and about in London, encouraging an interest in every aspect of life and answering questions with loving patience. He would meet friends and acquaintances from the worlds of politics and the arts, all enjoying an Indian summer of peace and prosperity. The family motored to Richmond Park for picnics on fine summer afternoons, whilst the Sunday programme became something of a tradition. In the morning the two Erskines visited St Paul's Cathedral, Westminster Abbey or Westminster Cathedral, followed in the afternoon by a 'wheel chair' walk with Molly and then an early evening concert at Queen's Hall or the Albert Hall from which developed a deep love of classical music.

Most summers, when their parents undertook expeditions in the *Asgard,* the boys were left in the care of their spinster aunts who lived near by in Chelsea. They usually had a week or two at an English south-coast resort but the undoubted highlight of the year was the visit to Ireland. Excited anticipation mounted until the morning when the family departed for Euston Station to join the train for Holyhead. Suddenly there was so much to see. A sweep of English countryside from the Home Counties across the Midlands, the landscape punctuated and scarred in places by industry, with trains in profusion at railway centres like Crewe and Chester. Embarkation was a special thrill, Irish accents suddenly seeming to predominate; and then some three hours out of Holyhead a first glimpse of the Wicklow Hills. At Kingstown (Dun Laoghaire) Robert Barton, known always as Uncle Bob, waited with his large white Daimler to convey the family on the final lap of the journey. As the car climbed up the side of the Great Sugar Loaf mountain above Kilmacanogue Erskine always imagined he was entering fairyland and the winding, lonely stretch of road through Calary retained an especial place in his affections.

At Glendalough House, the Barton home near Annamoe where his father had spent much of his own boyhood,

Erskine revelled in an environment totally different from the usual urban existence in London. Extensive grounds provided every challenge that a boy could desire. Fishing on Lough Dan proved more rewarding than Battersea Park lake whilst ascent of the Scar, a hill behind the house, remained a favourite even after he had tackled most mountains in these islands and many in Europe. With his father he explored the woodlands and discovered the great primeval roots and various mountain flowers and ferns found in the vicinity. Talking to the carpenter and the shepherd he learned of a way of life greatly at variance to his own.

Some of the visitors to Glendalough were prominent in Irish life, such as Sir Horace Plunkett, founder of the Irish Agricultural Organisation Society, and his associate George Russell, the poet, painter and mystic more usually known as AE, who intrigued Erskine from the time that they first met. On one occasion AE solemnly asked him if he could see the fairies, whereupon the boy apprehensively sought his mother's approval to do so!

Ireland of the Big House and the *ancien régime* in its last gasp of glory thus formed an important part of the backcloth to the early life of Erskine Childers. The Bartons derived much wealth from an ancestor who made a fortune in the wine business in France, were extensive landowners and staunchly Protestant. The menfolk were educated in Britain as tradition demanded. Yet in the years prior to the first World War they were by no means a typical Ascendency family. Robert Barton who had succeeded to the estate at the age of nine in 1890 was a product of Rugby, Christ Church, Oxford and the Royal Agricultural College at Cirencester. Striving hard to better the lot of staff and tenants, he was busy modernising properties and improving production by introducing modern farming techniques. An ardent Home Ruler like his cousin, he joined the National Volunteers in 1913 and acted for a spell as secretary to the Inspector General, Colonel Maurice Moore, who was a brother of the author George Moore.

Undoubtedly it was the influence of his parents which shaped Erskine's early life and thinking. Through them he came into contact with the beauty of nature, art, literature, music and poetry, from all of which he was to derive lasting comfort and joy. Apart from a brother five years his junior there were no other young children in the family and the predominance of adult company, combined with the fact that he was largely treated as a grown-up at home and encouraged to think for himself, meant that he matured ahead of his years throughout boyhood. Among the wider family he saw the Childers London aunts frequently and Barton cousins annually. But except for his Grandmother Osgood, who made frequent transatlantic visits after her husband's death, the American relatives were little more than names, though Christmas 1912 was spent in Paris, where the Osgoods and Warrens from New England shared the festivities with the Childers family from Old England.

In June 1914, during Erskine's final term at Mrs Spencer's school, his parents departed for their customary summer cruise and the aunts moved into the flat to keep an eye on the boys, though 'Flodgy' dealt with the more irksome chores. Telephone calls reassured them that all was well though Molly's brief letter from the Royal Marine Hotel at Cowes, indicating that 'you may not hear from us for a long time, perhaps two weeks', contained just a hint of mystery . Even if she had said that *Asgard* was in the process of running the gauntlet of the British Navy to deliver arms to the Irish Volunteers at Howth it would probably have been treated with amused disbelief. But a few weeks later while he was on holiday in the country Erskine was left in no doubt what was happening. 'Your father is going to war', Molly wrote, 'he has to go because he can do something no one else can for England.' Days later a letter arrived from his father asking him to take his place while he was away so that his mother could trust and rely on him. Quite a task for a boy not yet nine years old!

With his detailed knowledge of the North European

coastline it was inevitable that the services of the elder Childers were urgently sought by the Admiralty immediately war was declared and within days he was commissioned into the Royal Naval Air Service at Chatham. 'What a turn it is,' he wrote to his youngest sister Baa, 'all precedents overthrown, every balance upset, all normal life and habit and calculation thrown out of gear. Readjustment is deeply difficult for all of us, equanimity hard to attain.'[2]

In October 1914, as Erskine struggled for the first time with Latin and French at Gladstone's Preparatory School in Cliveden Place, Sloane Square, he heard again from his father reminding him of his responsibilities:

I hope you remember to be truthful and honourable ... to make Mother and me happy and proud of you and make us such friends with you that you hide nothing from us. You cannot be too loving to Mother these days, she is sad about the war and me being away. Oh, just pour out love and tenderness on her and take my place in doing things for her as much as you can, for remember you are the man of the family when I'm away and if she can trust you and lean on you think what joy it must give us.[3]

Childers senior was soon a trained observer, flying on reconnaisance and active missions from HMS *Engadine*, a primitive aircraft carrier hastily converted from a cross-Channel steamer, and celebrating Christmas Day by taking part in the first naval air raid in history — over Cuxhaven in *Riddle of the Sands* country.

Meanwhile in London the war at first impinged only marginally, though the absence of loved ones and friends and, after 1915, air raids and food shortages began to characterise life. Periodic excitement was aroused in the Childers household when Irish or American relatives called in for an evening on their way over to the Flanders front, some never to return. Despite her disability Molly plunged herself energetically into voluntary war work, becoming secretary of the Chelsea War Refugees Fund.

The work was largely connected with Belgian refugees, for whom Basil Williams was in charge of the reception arrangements at Folkestone. In the first months of the war she had contacted many infuential friends in a forlorn attempt to pressure the War Office to accept the Irish Volunteers as a fighting unit of the British Army in the same way as the Ulster Volunteers had been welcomed. Later she became Chairman and Treasurer of the Women Munition Workers' Rest Committee. Eventual award of an M.B.E. and a Belgian decoration was richly deserved but despite her dedicated commitment she urged her son to think objectively:

Don't hate any of our enemies. We have no enemies really. It's all a wicked game played by people at the top who don't care and never have cared for what happens to the poor workers and the miserable people. I hope England will win for I love her and don't want anyone but the English to rule England . . . Don't be afraid of anything . . . If there is need I am going to let you do some work to help England.[4]

Like most contemporary boys Erskine took a keen interest in various aspects of the war. Painstakingly he constructed a model destroyer based on technical advice from his father and in the park or on visits to the country played games such as 'Hill 60' or 'Neuve Chapelle' with innocent enjoyment. He wrote enthusiastically of a visit to an exhibition of trench mortars and German guns captured at Loos, but was forbidden to see a film about the Battle of the Somme which Molly thought to be too horrific. Periodic short stays in Felixstowe brought him into contact with the front line and he saw for himself the dangerous life his father was leading. While they were chatting together one day, a young pilot approached and non-chalantly informed the elder Erskine that lots had been drawn and he would be flying in an old Short seaplane which could not turn left! Testing times indeed for a man in his mid-forties, not to mention his nearest and dearest.

Despite their preoccupations both parents took the

keenest interest in Erskine's progress at school and endeavoured to ensure that his efforts matched the exacting standards they had set. Before his tenth birthday he had written a letter in Latin to his father, who corrected the grammar by return of post. During the long summer holidays in 1915 and 1916, while he was staying in the country, his mother made clear her expectations:

Are you working a full hour a day? Write to me one half-hour and do arithmetic for one half hour. Set yourself to it. All your life it will make a difference if, when you go back to school this time, you write and do your sums *exquisitely*. Do it for three reasons:
1) To be a great Englishman and help your country.
2) To be our pride and joy.
3) To be able to take pride in the beauty of your work.
You are a great lover of the beautiful. You love beautiful music, writing, pictures, sculpture, machines, inventions, nature, thoughts — seeing God in everything and worshipping him, characters, the people you love, father, grandmother, Aunt Gret, etc. I want you to be able to produce beauty in all you do ... Once you have seized hold upon an idea you always seem to be able to act upon it and make it your own.[5]

School reports showed a good all-round grasp of most subjects except drawing, in which he was usually bottom of the class, and in 1916 Mr Gladstone reported that Erskine's conduct was excellent and he had worked well.

It was natural that the Childers boys should long for their father's brief periods of leave, when their mother also would allow herself a respite. The harshness of war and separation increased the affection and longing each had for the other. In September 1916, after only a few days away from her elder son, Molly wrote from Felixstowe:

I am getting very lonely for you. Indeed today I am needing you especially badly. I would give much just to have you come running towards me and have you put your arms about me and kiss me. Each day that you grow older I find that I need you more and I am looking forward to a day which will come, please God,

14

when you will be a grown man, standing shoulder to shoulder with father and me, our equal and our friend in all things, as intimate with us as you know us to be with each other.[6]

With almost uncanny perception Molly knew when her husband was in danger and urged the boys to pray for his safety. Although both the elder Erskine's and Molly's views on organised religion were unorthodox they held an unshakable belief in a higher spiritual being. Certainly their creed was Christianly inspired. Indeed, reading correspondence between them one would assume they were a deeply religious couple in the conventional mould, Erskine had been taken to services in various London churches but never worshipped regularly or attended Sunday School or any other classes of instruction for fear that he would be tainted by denominational bigotry. God was to be worshipped under the sky rather than under a roof to a man-made set of rules. Yet spiritual matters undoubtedly figured prominently in long and intimate discussions with his parents.

In 1917 Lieut.-Commander Erskine Childers was awarded a D.S.O. for exceptional services and given a break from active duty. As an assistant secretary to Lloyd George's ill-fated Irish Convention, which met at Trinity College, Dublin from July onwards under the Chairmanship of Sir Horace Plunkett, he was suddenly thrust back into the cauldron of Irish politics. Confused at first by the happenings of Easter Week 1916, condemning the Rising as 'disgraceful',[7] Childers senior was equally confused by the actions of Robert Barton, who had resigned his Commission in the Royal Dublin Fusiliers and linked up with the Republicans. Once in Dublin it became obvious that even his long-advocated solution of Dominion status would be a compromise, so far had Sinn Féin (who officially boycotted the Convention) moved and gained in strength. Though the auguries for a successful outcome to the Convention were far from good there were personal compensations, Molly and Bobby being able to join him for several short stays in Dublin as the discussions dragged on for nine months. Renewed contact with Robert Barton gave opportunities for the cousins to thrash out the question of Ireland's future and one week-end at Glendalough House a lengthy discussion ended with the Englishman realising, perhaps for the first time, just how far the Republican movement had progressed.

With such food for thought combined with the unsatisfactory conclusion to the Convention itself, the inept bungling of the conscription issue by the British Government and the German 'plot' fiasco, the elder Erskine was in a state of mental turmoil about Ireland. Apart from a meeting with Sir Roger Casement in Belfast in October 1913, a man Molly thought half-crazed,[8] his first real contacts with the so-called revolutionary movement were made during the preparations for the Howth arms landing in July 1914. Then and since he had tended to regard the leaders as fanatics 'nourished on dreams'.[9] Now he could not be sure and it was with a sense of relief that he returned to London in April 1918. His initial posting was to the Air Ministry, for the R.N.A.S. had become a constituent of the recently formed Royal Air Force, in which he now held the rank of Major.

But young Erskine had more immediate worries in the first months of 1918. Overshadowing all else was the fact that his time at school in London was nearly over and he certainly did not relish the thought of leaving home for boarding-school. Life was especially happy at Gladstone's where he was a prefect. 'Don't be afraid of responsibility,' his father wrote from Dublin; 'it is sometimes hard not to be afraid but resolve and take it and use it for the good of the school and remember that to set a high example is now your bounden duty for without doing so you cannot command authority.'[10]

The choice of public school for their elder son had been the subject of much deliberation. The elder Erskine discounted Haileybury, his own school, whilst Lady Lyttelton, Molly's colleague on the Chelsea Refugee

Committee whose brother-in-law had been a distinguished Headmaster of Eton, urged that there could only be one choice. Though application was made to Uppingham and Rugby, a small but expanding sixteenth-century foundation in North Norfolk was ultimately selected. Gresham's School at Holt had grown from a purely local establishment and was acquiring an enviable academic reputation under an innovative Headmaster, G. W. S. Howson. He held liberal ideas and admired creative ability rather than theory, and Erskine's parents found much in common with him. But Erskine himself was, naturally, apprehensive and looked to the future with anything but equanimity as the time approached for his trunk to be packed.

Chapter II
IRELAND AND TRAGEDY

When Erskine Childers started at Gresham's School at the beginning of May 1918 his background and personal circumstances blended easily with those of most contemporaries. By the time he left six years later no other pupil could reasonably be expected to have shared either his recent experiences or his views on certain subjects. In very truth his life away from school had undergone a most traumatic upheaval for reasons which few could begin to comprehend.

The sixteen new boys who started at Gresham's for the summer term in 1918 shared with the other 220 pupils in the school one paramount desire — victory over Germany. None had escaped the shadow of war. Many had fathers serving in the forces, and some like Childers had both parents totally involved in the struggle, though Erskine had the immediate distinction of having the only 'flying' father.[1] Few had not lost a relative; all too regularly the assembled boys in chapel learned of a fresh name added to the Roll of Honour and the Holt War Loan effort was a source of pride. But over all, apart from the existence of ration books and a limited diet, the war did not greatly affect school life, nor indeed life in general in the rural spaciousness of North Norfolk.

Situated just to the east of the small town of Holt, Gresham's School straddles the road leading towards the seaside resorts of Sheringham and Cromer. Within five miles of the coast the air is sharp and bracing, and though the immediate environs of the school are well wooded there is a bleakness about the countryside for much of the year. Some 130 miles from London the railway journey was long and circuitous, involving several changes of train. The fastest expresses of the Midland and Great Northern Joint Line were regarded as slow everywhere else and there was no Sunday service. Small wonder that most new boys, away from home for the first time and struggling to adjust to strange surroundings, were overcome by a sense of utter isolation and bewilderment and Erskine proved no exception as he entered the junior school.

Loneliness dominated the early correspondence with his parents, who sometimes wrote three letters a day between them in an effort to comfort and console their son, tempering sympathy and understanding with practical advice. Recalling, perhaps, similar feelings in his own schooldays the elder Erskine wrote after a week or so:

You have been lonely, I'm afraid, and that could not be otherwise away from your home and dear ones but if you work hard, play hard, have many interests and a full, strenuous life and never cease loving and thinking of us here — Mother, me, Bobby and Floggie — you will be a happy boy ... In cricket will you remember that when you are batting and the bowler bowls to you, you must *never move* your left foot even if the ball is coming right at your body. Hold your ground and never run away from the ball. Just pivot your left foot and hit it as best you can.[2]

A day or two later, after Erskine had said that he would waste away, Molly followed up reassuringly:

My friendship is always waiting for you to need it — just waiting for you to call on it and now you are calling it all the time and I know at last that you need us as we need you, not just because we are Father, Mother and son but for a deeper reason still, a reason which is made up of what is spiritual and eternal. I know that we are bound up by the greatest bond of all and that is the miracle of Father's and my wonderful union, you have your place as part of it all with us. As years go by and you grow to be a man this will grow greater and greater until you will be beside

19

us, shoulder to shoulder, bearing the yoke of life with us. And our love will be beyond telling.[3]

As the first long term dragged by the loneliness started slowly to abate, though Erskine could still cite the hours, minutes and days before he would be reunited with his family. Particularly welcome and looked forward to was the first visit from his father at the end of June, after which the latter was able to write reassuringly to his sister that 'little E is happy and well and loving his school life now that his loneliness has gone'.[4] By the end of term he was an Old School House prefect and had enrolled as a Boy Scout. His first report was fairly good and very good in turns, mathematics being a particularly weak subject.

During the autumn term of 1918 Childers *père* was attached to RAF Group 27 at Bircham Newton in West Norfolk and visited his son again in most unconventional fashion. Erskine had pleaded with him to fly over the school and drop something for the boys. Shortly after the Armistice, doubtless by prior arrangement with the Head-master, the pupils were amazed early one morning to see an aeroplane taxi to a halt on the cricket field. As the two Erskines walked together into chapel their feelings of mutual delight and pride may be well imagined.

As the Childers family celebrated the first peaceful Christmas and Erskine experimented with his new Meccano outfit, the atmosphere in their Chelsea home was superficially relaxed, relieved and carefree. But Molly was deeply anxious for she knew that her husband, soon to be demobilised, was seriously contemplating removal to Ireland to give himself wholly to the struggle developing there. Ever since the collapse of the Convention nine months before, Irish affairs had rested heavily on him and the results of the December 1918 general election confirmed his belief that rule by Sinn Féin was inevitable due to the 'follies, betrayal and crimes of English policy'.[5] No fewer than 73 of the 105 Irish constituencies returned Sinn Féin members to Westminster on an abstentionist ticket, among them Robert Barton in West Wicklow, shortly to become Minister for Agriculture in the first Dáil which was established in January 1919.

Fate decreed that the elder Childers spent several weeks at Glendalough in the spring of 1919. After completing his final Royal Air Force assignment and surviving a nearly fatal attack of influenza he repaired there to recuperate and was immediately brought into contact with the harsher realities of Irish life. Robert Barton was on the run like a common criminal. Arrested for making what the British authorities described as a seditious speech at Carnew in his constituency, he succeeded in escaping from Mountjoy Prison, Dublin whilst awaiting trial. As his strength gradually returned Erskine's father was called upon to help manage the estate in his cousin's enforced absence and began renewing acquaintance with old friends such as AE and Edward Lysaght, who urged him to settle in Ireland.

Another Barton cousin, Dulcibella (Da), was deeply involved in the Sinn Féin struggle too, thinking nothing of riding a primitive motor cycle across the Wicklow Hills in the dead of night carrying despatches. To this atmosphere were added clandestine meetings with Barton himself and through him introductions to Michael Collins and Eamon de Valera, the President of both Sinn Féin and Dáil Éireann, who was soon to depart for an American tour. Both these influential figures established an instant rapport with Childers senior so that by the time he returned to Molly in London the die was virtually cast.

For Erskine change, or the prospect of it, characterised 1919. In January, Headmaster Howson died only a few days after Erskine had moved into Woodlands House in the senior school. His successor, James R. Eccles, the Woodlands Housemaster, had been on the staff since 1900 and was cast in a similar liberal mould, so that academic life was relatively undisturbed. But with the move to Dublin all but decided upon the long summer vacation provided a last gasp of the old, familiar London existence. For much of the time his father was home too, between spells in Paris endeavouring to publicise the Irish case at the Versailles Peace Conference, and the family even managed a holiday together at Worthing.

Evidence suggests that all aspects of a move across the Irish Sea were carefully considered, though Molly acquiesced only reluctantly at first. Childers senior knew the importance of the right environment. Earlier in 1919 he questioned the wisdom of his sister Constance (Baa) in moving from London to a village in Sussex lest she might not be suited to her new surroundings. He fully accepted that his son's education should continue in England. To arguments that his reasons for joining the Republican cause might be misunderstood he countered that Robert Barton had exactly the same antecedents, yet nobody apparently questioned his motives. He simply could not appreciate that any lasting detrimental effect might result for his family — for himself, of course, he was only too happy to face the consequences, whatever they might be. The decision was taken for better — or worse.

Already mature beyond his years Erskine understood his parents' wish to devote themselves to the cause of Irish independence, though the full implications were to evolve slowly over a number of years. As Ireland had always meant something special to him, he was angry to learn of British repression and injustice and proud to think of himself as an Irishman. Even so the rented villa in Wellington Road, Ballsbridge to which he travelled for the 1919 Christmas holiday contrasted unfavourably with the familiar surroundings of the flat in Embankment Gardens, Chelsea. The tense atmosphere of Dublin itself was markedly different too from the relaxed peace of the Irish countryside which he could recall from pre-war visits to Glendalough. But the presence of a great aunt from London and the beloved Flodgy was reassuring. The latter stayed in Dublin for some weeks assisting the Childers family to settle in after the move.

Erskine Childers senior was deeply immersed in publicity work for Sinn Féin. Despite the reservations of Arthur Griffith and others who found an intellectual conversion by a relative outsider difficult to understand, there were many more who recognised the value of this expert publicist, whatever his background, and the subsequent rise to prominence was rapid. On the nomination of Collins he was made an inaugural Director of the Republican Land Bank, which involved extensive travelling, and he also became Chairman of Rathmines – Pembroke Republican Justices, whilst Molly acted as a Trustee of the Republican Loan Fund. By the summer of 1920 the Childers family was installed in its own home at 12 Bushy Park Road, almost opposite Zion Parish Church in Rathgar, then the southern perimeter of Dublin's suburbia. The house soon became a mecca for journalists from far and near as the elder Erskine and Molly sought to inform the world of the vicious reprisals perpetrated by British auxiliaries and 'black and tans' recruited by Lloyd George to stamp out what he termed the 'murder gang'. A small band of Liberal M.P.s at Westminster and some sympathetic Senators in Washington were kept faithfully advised of the steady, sorry catalogue of sordid events during 1920 and 1921 and some telling articles were penned by Childers for British and American journals.

After the first unhappy term at Gresham's Erskine and his parents normally corresponded once a week. His letters during the period 1919 to 1922 reflect a developing mind and were in many respects what might be expected from an English public schoolboy of the period. Consistently he requested jam to be sent — redcurrant, blackberry and raspberry being the favourite flavours. Some of the terminology sounds quaintly dated: 'thanks awfully for those apples', he wrote on one occasion, 'they are absolutely ripping.' A microscope was asked for to assist with scientific experiments, ambition at this time lying in the direction of medicine. *Irish Nationality* by Alice Stopford Green, *The Black Tulip* by Dumas and *Gods and Fighting Men* by Lady Gregory were among books which gave especial pleasure and he quoted schoolboy doggerel:

Erskine Childers sat on a wall,
Erskine Childers had a great fall,
Beakers and bromide and sulphates of lead,
Couldn't mend poor little Erskine's head,

as easily as more serious verse, such as Shelley on death:

First our pleasures die and then
Our hopes and then our fears and when
These are dead the debt is due.

At the age of sixteen he confessed to enjoying *Exultation* by Montague Phillips and the Gilbert and Sullivan operas, and he was just beginning to appreciate Beethoven but found modern music difficult to listen to.[6]

Letters from Ireland combined advice on scholastic matters with general information on political affairs. For instance Erskine senior wrote (20 September 1920), 'Don't take extra chemistry but extra Latin. Chemistry can be learned at any age and is not education to the mind. Latin is and must be learned young. The soldiers and black and tans are becoming appalling.' There can be little doubt that Erskine missed parental visits such as most of the other boys enjoyed once or twice a term. His Childers aunts visited Holt infrequently and at least once his grandmother, Mrs Osgood, and Aunt Gretchen (Molly's sister from Boston) called, the latter doubtless leaving Headmaster Eccles in no doubt about her views on her relative's latter-day politics. From the start she had strongly opposed the family's close involvement with Sinn Féin.

Returning home for the school holidays Erskine learned at first hand of the ruthless excesses of the black-and-tans, of raids on his parents' house, of Robert Barton serving ten years' imprisonment at Portland for a speech which was mild compared with the threats uttered with apparent impunity by Carson and others before 1914, so that at the age of fifteen he was afire with Republicanism. There were still occasional family evenings when his parents recited poetry and reminisced about happy times in the past. They spoke at length about Erskine's difficulties at school where few could appreciate his position, urging him to love and respect his fellows, to help them and be thoughtful, to be gentle in argument and not to hurt anyone. On a typical day though, the two Erskines met at breakfast and thereafter only fleetingly. The younger was aware of the enormous pressures on his father and saw him ageing beyond his years, thin and drawn, his countenance becoming mournful with much of the old humour and sparkle draining away. A troublesome cough, legacy from the influenza, refused to be cured. Ever a slave of duty, when at home he was usually working upstairs in his small office, writing, writing, writing.

Members of Sinn Féin, prominent and not so prominent, sought sanctuary at 12 Bushy Park Road before the house was declared 'unsafe'. Desmond Fitzgerald, Robert Brennan and Frank Gallagher were among the most regular visitors. Taking his cue from his parents Erskine sometimes chatted with impressive authority to a waiting journalist, revealing great knowledge of Irish affairs. Many of his cycle rides around Dublin had deeper significance than simple sightseeing. The most vigilant auxiliary would hesitate to question a youngster on a bicycle delivering a letter. Occasional sorties into the mountains for a secret rendezvous added extra spice. Could there have been another schoolboy in England at this period who spent his holidays in such a manner?

Just before the Childers family moved from London J. R. Eccles spent a day with Erskine senior and Molly and impressed them greatly with his 'large mind and heart, sympathy and understanding and noble standards'. They believed that 'there is no school like Holt and no house like his house in England'. Even if he was bemused by the desire to uproot and help what he regarded as the rebel Irish cause he could not doubt the sincerity of purpose. Eccles sometimes sent for Erskine to discuss the latest developments in Ireland, reading an occasional issue of the

25

Irish Bulletin which the elder Childers edited. Not long after he had complained that 'J. R. E. is always introducing me as a sort of curiosity i.e. Sinn Féin, he is awfully nice about it', Erskine was writing; 'J. R. E. has changed sadly, he wants independence but thinks the I.R.A. are all brigands and must be rooted out before the British Army is withdrawn.'

To the eyes of the boys who shared Woodlands House dormitory there was something incongruous about the photograph of Eamon de Valera which appeared on Erskine's bedside locker and the owner was the first to admit that Gresham's was probably the only public school in England where it would be permitted. This was the outward manifestation of his pride that, next to his father, the President of the Irish Republic was now his greatest hero as well as Head of the State to which his allegiance belonged. Such a sudden transition was too much for his schoolfellows, who perceived nothing remotely Irish in Childers. Wasn't his father English and his mother American, they would say amongst themselves. Several other boys had Irish relatives but surely this Republican nonsense was being taken too far!

Initially the teasing was treated rather too seriously. Erskine would rise instantly to the bait of a casual taunt such as 'black and tan', letting words pour from his mouth to the amusement of the other boys. He heaped some of the trouble upon himself by exasperating even his friends almost past endurance with what sounded to them like extraordinary political views. But like his father, and remembering his advice, he never became in the least abusive or discourteous and always succeeded in preserving a certain detachment.[7] Paradoxically, whereas in the Dáil it was the elder Erskine's suave, unemotional manner and cultured accent which jarred with some deputies, rather than the content of his speeches, in the school dormitory the position was the reverse.

There were times when Erskine was confused himself by conflicting loyalties. His father became Minister of Publicity following the arrest and imprisonment of

Desmond Fitzgerald in February 1921 and thereafter the house in Bushy Park Road was kept under ever closer surveillance. After a raid in May the new Minister was arrested and taken to Dublin Castle for questioning. Although he was held for only a few hours his son was greatly upset by news of the arrest and wrote immediately to Lady Courtney, a family friend and former Chelsea neighbour, urging her to use her influence to obtain his father's release. Molly's reaction was perhaps predictable:

How can we ask help like that because we are highly placed when our fellow workers have no such power to save them from being tortured, thrown into prison and kept there for years. We are now Irish citizens and our work is to get recognition as such. Why should we alone escape the consequences. Does not the thought make you feel shame.

In May 1921 Childers senior was elected unopposed as one of the panel of five Sinn Féin deputies for Kildare – Wicklow and entered the Dáil for the most crowded and crucial year of his life. Selected to accompany the Irish party to London after the Truce in July he was now in the forefront of what were regarded in Britain as the Revolutionary politics of its sister island — and this after less than two years of residence in Ireland. But as he worked at Grosvenor House backing up de Valera in his discussions with Lloyd George his son had problems of a different kind. Like most of his schoolfellows he was anxious to attend a Public Schools Officer Training Corps camp at Strensall near York, but called off the project rapidly after receiving another stern rebuke from his mother:

You certainly cannot go to a British Military School camp — unless you here and now give up your whole position about Ireland. The thing is incredible to me. Do you realise that the whole purpose of the military side is to make you a British soldier. The whole question of your going to Holt has been difficult but if you do this thing I think father will say that he can no longer let you go there ... If you choose you can be English

27

— fight for England against us. You cannot be both S.F. and go to that camp in honour and wear that uniform even for one moment. To wear that uniform even for ten days means you support British Military policy. Father is back in London with the President. I shall not send your letter to him he is so overworked it might be the last straw. You must choose honourably — one or the other. Aunt Gret would say the same but she would ask you to be British and tell you Father and I and Uncle Bob and Bobby all would deserve to go to prison if we did not now surrender and accept Lloyd George's maximum offer.

Even the hoped-for consolation of a visit from his father and 'uncle' while they were in London failed to materialise. The consequences of being the son of revolutionaries were becoming more apparent day by day.

If his rise to fame in Irish politics was nothing short of meteoric the elder Erskine's fall from grace was no less so. By the winter of 1921–2 life was beginning to turn sour as the worst fears of English friends began slowly to be realised. The Treaty negotiations, where he acted as secretary to the Irish Delegation of Plenipotentiaries, found him in London for many weeks during October and November 1921. 'Do not think that I am not watching anxiously for a chance of coming to see you', he wrote to Erskine, who replied with detailed lists of train times, names of car-hire firms in Cromer and an offer to arrange accommodation in Sheringham. But the chance never came and despite his acute disappointment Erskine was able to write:

I realise what a wonderful father I have and what he has done for me as well as for the world and I also love that father more passionately than anything conceivable in the world. Every term I go away I realise more and more what you and Mother are to me. And nothing you have ever said gets forgotten ... I only hope that I can reward all you have done for me by doing something great for the world, it is a very hard thing to do in service.

28

After the signing of the Anglo-Irish Treaty on 6 December 1921, by which time Griffith and Collins were showing open hostility to his father, Erskine enquired anxiously:

What is going to happen about Dev? I do hope they avoid a schism. Which side is father? Anyway they will abide by the country's decision won't they? We must have a special Christmas for peace. Everything is so different here in Norfolk from Ireland. There is no real spirit in the country as there is in Wicklow . . . each village you go through is sleepier than the last.

Alas for the hopes of unity. Childers *père* spent much of the Christmas holiday working on Document No. 2, the Republican answer to the problem of the Oath of Allegiance to the English throne, and was roundly abused by the *Freeman's Journal* a few days later. Subsequent acrimonious Dáil debates prompted adverse press reaction to the Englishman's implacable opposition to the Dominion status which he had himself previously advocated. He was also blamed for the fact that Robert Barton, a Treaty signatory, rejected the document once he had honoured his commitment to vote for it. Arthur Griffith thumped the table saying that he would not reply to a 'damned Englishman' who, he implied, was an English Secret Service Agent.[8] An Ireland hungry for peace had little time for seemingly niggling theories about the Oath. Finally the electors of Kildare–Wicklow rejected him at the general election in June 1922. Not long before school broke up for the summer holiday Erskine received a short letter from his father, little dreaming that it would be the last:

I am working for the Republic in the war. I am sure you will understand what it all means and read through the lies of the English papers. I know how you are feeling, all about it. It's such a passionate joy that our boy is with us and will carry the torch when we are gone.

By the time he arrived home his father had already left and was acting as a non-combatant staff captain with the

29

I.R.A. (the military wing of the Republican anti-Treaty faction of Sinn Féin) in Munster, editing and publishing its war journal often under difficult, even hazardous conditions.

As brother faced brother, families divided and treachery thrived in all the horror of civil war, the elder Childers began to be falsely associated with many of the incidents reported almost daily in the Irish and British press. The Provisional Government became ruthless in its determination to stamp out Republican armed resistance and Home Affairs Minister Kevin O'Higgins spoke ominously in the Dáil of 'the able Englishman who is leading those ... opposed to this Government ... steadily, callously and ghoulishly ... striking at the heart of this nation, striking deadly, or what he hopes are deadly, blows at the economic life of this nation'.[9] Character assassination had never been more vicious as Childers senior fell victim of propaganda quite as deadly as anything emanating from his own pen.

Never had Erskine returned to school more reluctantly than for the Michaelmas term in 1922. It was difficult to concentrate on study when the father whom he adored and worshipped almost as a saint was in danger for his life, physically near to exhaustion, his ideals shattered. Mention of the name which he himself bore caused nostrils to twitch. Few in England, let alone at Gresham's School, could be expected to understand. There was, perhaps, some compensation in the fact that the young Erskine had a new study companion, the Hon. Mervyn Roberts, younger son of Lord Clwyd who as J. H. Roberts had sat in Parliament as the Liberal Member for West Denbighshire from 1892 until 1918. He had taken part in the eighty-two sittings devoted to Gladstone's second Irish Home Rule Bill for which he voted in 1893. To this day Mr Roberts cannot be sure of the reason why Erskine asked him, as he was a year younger and, in his own words, a backward introvert obsessively interested in music and the arts but little else. A missionary instinct, always latent, was evident in Erskine's explanation to his mother:

Roberts is a boy whom you have to draw out. Delicacy of health
has made him very shy and reserved and without much esprit de
corps. But when I got to know him I realised that there is a great
deal in him which one does not see at first. He and I agree on a
great many things, absolutely on Ireland. He is a prodigy at
music and knows more about art and sculpture and architecture
than one could have imagined. We have struck up a real friendship together.

As the weeks dragged on through October Molly's
letters became less frequent and were invariably brief.
Though the contents were largely superficial a veneer of
normality was preserved as the possibility of Erskine's
sitting for the Cambridge University preliminary examination was mooted. An entrance form was completed but
his mother urged him to delay for a year as 'life should
settle down'. Then, suddenly, one day early in November
came a summons from the Headmaster, who informed him
of his father's arrest and told him to leave at once for
Dublin.

The consequences were as obvious to Erskine as they
were to virtually everyone else in Britain and Ireland, for
there could be only one end to a campaign of such fierce
and sustained denigration. Poignancy was added by the
fact that the arrest had taken place at Glendalough House
in the company of a childhood friend, David Robinson,
from a similar Anglo-Irish background. That the offence
itself was trivial, possession of a small Colt revolver —
ironically a gift from Michael Collins — mattered not.
Imposition of the death penalty for unlawful possession of
arms indicated the lengths to which the Provisional Free
State Government were prepared to go and, despite
valiant attempts by his lawyers, Erskine Childers senior
was among the first to receive the sentence by a Military
Court. Efforts by influential friends on both sides of the
Irish Sea proved of no avail.

Grudgingly the Free State authorities permitted Erskine

to visit his condemned father. Conversation in the small, dirty cell at Dublin's Portobello Barracks was difficult with a gas jet screaming out into the stale air and the eyes of the guards fixed firmly on the two occupants. Grey-haired, drawn and prematurely aged, obviously unwell, the older man spoke movingly to the son whom he would never see again. Conscious that he might for ever be synonymous with the fratricide of civil war he gave his last paternal wishes as part of an endeavour to counter this. Aware of the significance of the meeting Erskine listened intently as his father asked him if he was thinking of entering political life in Ireland. He then sought his son's promise never to refer to the Civil War and to do everything possible to effect reconciliation between Irishmen and between Britain and Ireland, urging him to approach those who had signed his death-warrant and personally convey his forgiveness, a daunting task which was faithfully undertaken. [10]

The elder Childers prepared the way for his son by ensuring that every action during his last days pointed to reconciliation. He even shook hands with the firing-squad at Beggars Bush Barracks just after dawn on 24 November and then called them to come closer in an effort to ease their burden. When confirmation of the inevitable execution reached Molly around mid-morning she calmly conveyed the news to her sons and Erskine recalled this as the most poignant moment in the whole trauma. His own reaction was instantaneous, declaring firmly that 'the Republic will go on', a statement which shocked the artist Jack B. Yeats when he called at the house to express sympathy. [11]

The healing words of his father and his mother's supreme example helped Erskine to overcome the instincts of bitterness and hate which would quite naturally colour the thinking of most seventeen-year-old boys in similar circumstances. He determined that the name Erskine Childers would one day be associated with peace and harmony and restored to a place of honour with all harsh memories of conflict erased.

Chapter III
REVERBERATIONS AND ROMANCE

Nowhere had the dramatic events surrounding the arrest and execution of Robert Erskine Childers been watched with keener interest than at Gresham's School. Most people in England were probably more ready to accept Winston Churchill's description of him as a murderous renegade than de Valera's as a prince among men or Gavan Duffy's Dáil statement that he was one of the noblest men that he had known. Obituary notices in English newspapers were largely uncomplimentary. Whilst some extolled his work for England and expressed bewilderment about the latter stage of his life, others were merely contemptuous.

The Gresham's Governors received several approaches from parents who wondered if their sons might be contaminated by associating with the son of such a man and pondered momentarily whether Erskine should be asked to leave. However, Headmaster Eccles reminded them that when he came to the school his father was in the R.A.F. and the boy should not suffer for his subsequent actions. Furthermore, he assembled the boys of Woodlands House and urged them to welcome Erskine back, pointing out that he would be a very unnatural son if he was not loyal to his father, even to his politics.

One of Erskine's abortive attempts to influence the political thinking of his schoolfellows concerned the occupant of the next bed in the dormitory. Humphrey Whistler, of Irish descent himself, retains a vivid memory of the night Childers returned to school, deeply and profoundly shaken yet sleeping peacefully. English reserve prevented Whistler, later an Anglican Priest, from extending even warmer sympathy as he tried to imagine what it must have been like to say goodbye to one's father in such awful circumstances. More than a few boys felt touches of remorse and all baiting ceased forthwith as the human aspect of the tragedy overshadowed all others. Quietly and with no overt indications of bitterness, the threads of school life were taken up and Erskine won the admiration of staff and pupils in the process. The spirit of forgiveness and courage which he displayed was no more, no less than his father would have expected.[1]

When the *Glasgow Herald* reported Erskine's presence at his father's trial, sitting at the back of Green Street court with his aunts, it described him accurately as a good-looking typical English public-school boy.[2] The general impression in his late teens was undeniably appealing: clear, candid blue eyes which held one fixedly whilst in conversation, a fresh complexion, good features and thick fair hair which was worn rather long for the period, yet never seeming untidy despite a habit of pushing his fingers through it when preoccupied. His rather large head earned him the nickname 'Bong' which was unconsciously apt and stuck throughout his schooldays. Always friendly and helpful, to younger boys as well, he could sometimes be secretive despite a basically extrovert character.[3]

The last few weeks of 1922 could hardly be expected to be happy ones. His father dead, his mother ailing, many hopes and dreams shattered, the immediate prospect of a quiet Christmas in Sussex with his widowed Aunt Baa offered little comfort, for she had never understood the move to Ireland. Conscious of this Molly made it clear that despite the trauma she expected Erskine to put the happiness of others first: 'I want you to tend Baa and give her great joy. Be gentle and do not argue as you sometimes do. Be receptive to the ideas of others even while holding your own. You are going to be a great man in great ways.'

During the holiday Erksine borrowed a Ford car from the

local village garage and after only a few days tuition proved his ability behind the steering-wheel. He took pride in the handwritten certificate of competence given by the proprietor of Chailey Garage, obtained less than a month after his seventeenth birthday. On the way back to Holt he stopped in London to meet his grandmother, who had just arrived from the United States *en route* to Dublin to comfort her widowed daughter. For a visit to the British Museum they were joined by a young American lady, Miss Ruth Ellen Dow from Exeter, New Hampshire, whom Mrs Osgood had befriended aboard the S.S. *Olympic* during the passage from New York. Erskine and Ruth found an immediate rapport and as they walked along the Strand back to the Savoy Hotel where Ruth was staying, Erskine was conscious of an emotion that he had not hitherto experienced.

At first glance the sophisticated twenty-three-year-old transatlantic visitor and the English schoolboy were an improbable pair, yet fate decreed that they met at precisely the time that each was searching to fill a deep void in their lives. Ruth, a social-science graduate from Wellesley College, Massachusetts, having broken off her engagement, had left her old life behind to accompany the estranged wife of a wealthy Philadelphia business tycoon on a tour of Europe. Learning from Mrs Osgood the story of the Childerses' involvement in Irish politics she was patently intrigued to meet the Erskine who, only seven weeks after the loss of his father and still in a state of numbed shock, warmed at once to the New Englander's cheerful chatter with its underlying tone of deep thought and understanding.

Thus began a friendship which was to grow and flourish, initially by way of correspondence, Erskine writing from the somewhat spartan school study and Ruth from one of the plush Savoy lounges overlooking the Thames. The former wrote enthusiastically to his mother, 'the more I know her the gladder I am I met her', and Ruth herself made an approach to Molly soon afterwards:

Ever since I have met Erskine I have wanted to write and tell you what it is to know such a boy and what an inspiration it is to feel his father's spirit and yours through him. It has lifted me far out of my tiny self and made me wish that tiny self could in some way help you, for your sacrifice has been so glorious. I am with you. Someday I long to come to Ireland and know Erskine's wonderful mother.

Molly responded by return:

How I rejoice to get your letter for which I was hoping. You have brought great happiness by all your kindness to our boy. He has written of you as being his first girl friend and has told me things of you which — how can I say it — I would have prayed he would find in every friendship he makes. I cannot say more than that. He is reserved although so eager in meeting his fellow beings and I know by what he has written that you have really helped him at a time when he needed to make such a friend.

The reply delighted Ruth who wrote excitedly to Erskine, 'Doesn't it make your heart sing underneath, really sing, to be able to have her together to serve and make happy and keep with all our powers from any more suffering ... I long to fly to her.'

In the first weeks of 1923 Ruth's duties took her to Brighton and Paris but she visited Dublin on her own at the end of March, establishing an immediate rapport with Molly Childers. With deep New England roots like the Osgoods — Henry Dow from Ormsby, Norfolk settled at Hampton, New Hampshire in 1644 to become one of the State's most influential early figures — an affinity between the two ladies was readily apparent. The Congregational Church at Exeter, N.H. provided a tangible link between the two families for, whereas an Osgood ancestor was a founder member, the Dows traced descent from the second Pastor. Now Ruth pondered whether or not to return to America, deciding without too much prompting to stay in England. However, it was Ireland which caught her imagination, in particular the political situation and the influence of the Roman Catholic Church. 'Why does it almost always happen', she asked Erskine, 'that people — Protestants — who make Ireland their deepest dream always turn towards the Catholic faith?[9]

During her short stay in Dublin while the Civil War was still in progress Ruth undertook a couple of assignments in connection with Molly's publicity work for Sinn Féin. Wearing a plaid raincoat she visited the University Church in St Stephen's Green and after kneeling at the altar rail for several minutes was conscious of a bundle of papers being surreptitiously slipped under her arm. This and other clandestine tasks were undertaken with an attitude of adventurous detachment but it was beginning to crystallise into one of commitment by the time she left.

To an already schizophrenic existence of academic life in England and Republican politics in Ireland two further responsibilities now competed for the time and attention of the very youthful Erskine. As the elder son he knew how his mother relied on him to take his father's place, even urging him to think of himself as 'father'. At the same time the relationship with Ruth tended more and more to dominate his thoughts and led to intimate and lengthy letters. The letters prompted his mother to remind him that his brother and grandmother — and by implication herself — should always take precedence over the friendship. Whilst Molly genuinely welcomed it she had reservations that her son might be getting too involved and could eventually be hurt.

The correspondence between Erskine and Ruth was prolific. They discussed sin, suffering, separation, emotions, fulfilment and nature, and frequently quoted poetry, prose and prayers. Almost patronisingly Erskine once commented that Ruth's letters had a strength of purpose about them and provided an interesting study in mental evolution. Religion and spiritual matters were a regularly recurring topic during 1923 and 1924. Ruth thought Erskine would make a wonderful Minister! But despite a visit to the Vatican with his grandmother at Easter 1923, when he was received in audience by Pope Pius XI, he was quite unmoved by Ruth's sudden leaning towards Catholicism, suggesting that Buddhism had more to offer. 'Your religion sounds frightfully mixed up, dear', she responded; 'do you know what you believe?' Above all, it was dogma and doctrine that he rejected and this applied to the Anglican Church as well. Although much impressed by the beauty of a Confirmation service in the School Chapel he told his mother that he could not take Communion as he did not believe in the Creed or the 39 Articles, a view reflecting exactly his parents, somewhat unorthodox teaching. Before long there was another topic on which Erskine disagreed with Ruth, for in May 1923 she had taken a job in London as a secretary in the office of Shaphurji Saklatvala, the Parsee Communist M.P. for Battersea North.

A Britain examining its racial conscience in the latter part of the twentieth century may have forgotten that the first coloured member was elected to Parliament in 1892, the same year as Keir Hardie. Saklatvala was, in fact, the third Indian and the second Communist to sit at Westminster, having been returned on a Labour ticket in 1922. His first action in the Commons was to move rejection of the Irish Constitution Bill. A previous Labour candidate in Battersea North, Mrs Charlotte Despard, was by this time fighting for the Republican cause in Dublin. Much of Ruth's work for Saklatvala was connected with efforts to secure better conditions for colonial workers in England, but Erskine said that Communism was the happy hunting-ground for cranks and twitted her for singing *The Red Flag*. Back in New Hampshire the Dow parents were genuinely appalled by their daughter's involvement with Communism and Roman Catholicism (there is no record of their views on Irish Republicanism!) and refused point-blank to consider financing further study at Cambridge which Ruth briefly thought of undertaking.

Meanwhile in Ireland the resistance of the Republican

military wing spluttered on ever more ineffectually and sporadically throughout the winter of 1922/23 before operations were officially suspended after the shooting of Liam Lynch. Peace was restored at a heavy price. Eighty-two Republicans had been executed by the Free State in six months, while many more were imprisoned and some 2000 were fugitives in hiding. The latter included Eamon de Valera, still President of the Republic and Sinn Féin. There was a fear that those captured might be murdered without trial. Molly Childers remained in the thick of things, continuing publicity work and editing a news-sheet of sorts which played a vital role in keeping the political organisation of Sinn Féin intact in the knowledge that the Government would soon seek a fresh mandate.

Fortuitously the August 1923 Irish General Election, first to be held under the new franchise provided by Article 15 of the Constitution, coincided with the school holiday when Erskine was home for the first time in nearly nine months. With Robert Barton in gaol he was anxious to join the campaign in Wicklow, but de Valera was reluctant to allow overt campaigning for fear that more arrests would be made by the Free State authorities. Erskine wrote to the President:

Mother has told me of your decision in the matter of political work. Will you kindly tell me if you could alter it if the Free State continues to leave electioneering officials untouched? As you can guess I long to do work and having to live 'meekly' in the Free State is very hard to bear!! The particular work I am thinking of is for Miss Barton in County Wicklow where I could be of some service to her. Does this meet with your approval?

Before he could reply de Valera was himself arrested as he emerged from hiding to address an election rally at Ennis in his County Clare constituency on 16 August. This was a bitter blow to the depleted Republican ranks struggling to organise a campaign against overwhelming odds, even though any successful candidates would not take the Oath nor, in consequence, their seats in the Dáil.

With most of the leading opponents of the Treaty such as Patrick Ruttledge, Austin Stack, Dr James Ryan, Frank Aiken and Seán Lemass either in prison or in hiding, the ladies and youngsters of Sinn Féin bore the brunt of electioneering. At a large rally in O'Connell Street, Dublin on Sunday, 19 August 1923, Alderman Mrs Kathleen Clarke, widow of the 1916 hero, presided. Speakers included Dr Kathleen Lynn, member of a Protestant Ascendency family, and two schoolboys, Vivion de Valera, the ten-year-old eldest son of the President, and Erskine Childers. For the latter, making his first public oration, it was a welcome opportunity to reaffirm loyalty to his father's ideals and express disgust at events in Ennis a few days before. He was warmly received as he declared:

Republican comrades, in the name of Erskine Childers, my beloved father, I stand here to protest against the arrest of our President and great leader, Mr de Valera, a friend of every one of us. Does the Free State Government believe they are promoting peace when they take him away from us? Although we are deprived of his inspiring guidance we will remember his noble example and what he has taught us and will do all that in us lies by faithful labour and, if need be, by sacrifice to strengthen the Republic. I am thinking of my father and all Ireland's terrible losses in the past year, and I am thinking of the greatest leader Ireland has ever had to help her — the President. I ask you to pray night and day for his safety and that Ireland may never again be stained by the blood of her faithful sons.

When the votes were counted, the Republicans, surprisingly, had virtually held their ground by winning forty-four seats to the sixty-three of Cumann na Gaedheal, the pro-Treaty party. Though de Valera headed the poll in East Clare there was sadness in the Childers family at the narrow defeat of Robert Barton in Wicklow, but all in all Erskine could return to England content that his vacation had been well spent. The establishment of the Republic, if no nearer, was, by the same token, no further away.

At about this time in a long letter to Ruth he looked ahead to the sort of Ireland he hoped one day to see:

I shall fight tooth and nail against industrialising Ireland. Let her remain poor but let us never become complex. The people are simple and spiritual. That word prosperity, ugh! I shall not mind living in poverty if we can be simple. I so fear when the Republic comes that Irish capitalists will spring like mushrooms. If we cannot live in prosperity, on agriculture, then let us be poor. Blessed are the meek for they shall inherit the earth. Even if it means remaining without influence in a worldly sense let us remain simple. It is my interpretation of Christ — keeping this country from civilisation. Let us not talk about Ireland as Mussolini does of Italy. Oh, I hope people will not try to bring Ireland 'into line with the foremost nations of the earth'. Let her remain pure and simple in frugality. Then after much suffering when the rest of the world is rotting Ireland will take her place and lead the way. I dreamt I spoke at the Dáil about this when a grant for subsidising some huge industrial plant was put forward and they thought I was a fanatic!

Reports of the O'Connell Street rally were given prominence by the English press, and several newspapers featured pictures of Erskine standing on the rostrum clutching his notes. It was more than some members of the British establishment could bear and renewed pressure was put upon the Governors and Headmaster of Gresham's School. Eccles could stand it no longer and interviewed his 'revolutionary' pupil as soon as he returned to commence the autumn term. Although he had always been a credit to his house and school in the sense by which pupils are normally judged Erskine was told that the school had suffered and the Headmaster personally had suffered because of him. For this reason he could not be considered as house captain and furthermore must leave in July 1924, thereby forfeiting the chance of obtaining a scholarship to Cambridge. Further, his younger brother

Robert could not now be accepted as a pupil at Gresham's.

As the consequences of the elder Erskine's decision to adopt the Irish Republican cause marked the lives of his sons, predictions by English friends some five years before were proving all too accurate. Yet there is no indication that young Erskine reacted other than in an objective way, except perhaps with anger that his brother was suffering more than he ought. He was concerned that his Headmaster should not bear the brunt of the criticism from parents. Indeed, his affection and regard for him was undimmed and he wrote to his mother, 'J. R. E. is a wonderful person, thank goodness whatever the Governors may think or do, whatever J. R. E. may have had said to him by them, he still trusts me implicitly.'

Once the shock of the bitter disappointments began to abate the final school year started to prove enjoyable, especially after the Cambridge entrance examination had successfully been sat in November. He was accepted for himself and basked in a certain amount of glory by virtue of having a twenty-four-year old American girl friend. In May 1924, too late for any meaningful parental protest, he was appointed a prefect with responsibility for 48 boys. His first duty was to explain Gresham's unusual honour system, under which boys were trusted to obey the rules and own up when they broke them, to the new entrants — doubtless reflecting that his brother should have been among them.

The Childers–Roberts study became something of a salon for the school's literary 'élite' which included a precocious younger pupil, Wystan H. Auden. Roberts recalls his companion's enthusiasm for the poetry of Blake and Shelley together with AE's mystical verse and the common ground that they shared in the realm of religio-philosophic speculation. Two books of especial value to Erskine at this period were *A Greek View of Life* by Professor Lowes Dickinson of King's College, Cambridge and *The Condition of Man* by an American philosopher-scientist, Alexis Carrel.

Though he was not outstanding academically Erskine's range of subjects included humanities and science and he was top of the school in English. Athletically, although gaining his hockey colours, his great love was always cycling. The combination of a powerful three-speed gear and energetic pedalling proved exhausting to companions and he often traversed the quiet Norfolk lanes on his own, enjoying the scenery and exploring countless village churches, pondering on the past and speculating about the future. [4]

Among the broader range of school activities was the Sociological Society which, according to W. H. Auden, had been formed to provide an excuse to have a grand time visiting factories in a charabanc. [5] Certainly Erskine enjoyed these visits, Colman's Mustard Factory and the Great Eastern Railway depot in Norwich giving him a brief insight into industrial life with which he was previously unacquainted. During their final term senior pupils spent some time at a Boys Club in Lowestoft which was adopted as the school 'mission'. Games were organised, and impromptu and very amateur entertainment was provided for the less privileged youngsters.

A debate at Gresham's League of Nations Union in May 1924 found Erskine at the centre of a controversy which had no connection with Ireland. He proposed a resolution condemning the British Government for breach of Article 8 of the League Covenant for its intended purchase of a death-ray machine which, reputedly, could cause internal disease, stop machinery and destroy life. Reports in national newspapers had fuelled speculation over claims by its inventor, H. Grindell-Matthews, that the device enabled power to be transmitted through the air from point to point by means of light rays. However, a demonstration given to Air Ministry officials proved inconclusive and little more was heard of the project. The Gresham's resolution was defeated but Erskine won admiration for his presentation of the case and drew especial comfort from the remark of one schoolfellow. 'Childers,' he said, 'I think

I understand now what you feel like in Ireland, everybody against you yet you feel so proud to be in a minority.'

Just three weeks before school life ended Erskine summed it all up in a letter to Ruth:

It is ending very peacefully and happily, a little life in itself. At first wonder and overwhelming home sickness, then gradual learning, then the screw turning and antagonism and now victory and peace and such happiness as I never knew. When I look back on the last five years they have been very full with a good deal to face ... Above all I have learned the real heart of England in a way only a few in Ireland will ever know. For that alone I would have come here.

Maturity and self-discipline, poise and reliability, are words that recur when contemporaries recall Erskine Childers's time at school. Though parental influence was paramount in shaping his attitudes and outlook Gresham's and in particular the Headmaster deserve credit for a not inconsiderable part in the moulding of his character. Stability and continuity had been provided at a time when his domestic circumstances altered radically and tragically. He was allowed to develop relatively unhindered as his own man without the rigidity and sterner discipline associated with the traditional public-school education. The tolerance and faith of J. R. Eccles, though questioned by others, was invaluable in sustaining confidence at a time when it was most needed.

As he cycled from Holt for the last time, across the Midlands of England and North Wales en route to Dublin in early August 1924, the young Childers, whose self-professed key to life was 'Ireland first, Ireland last and Ireland all the way', was in most obvious respects an Englishman, blending more readily with the populace of King's Lynn or Derby than he ever would with the people of Kilkenny or Drogheda.

Chapter IV
AN UNUSUAL UNDERGRADUATE

One year earlier than envisaged, in October 1924, Erskine Childers passed through the Great Gate of Trinity College, Cambridge and was at once walking more closely in the shadow of his father. Most of the forty or so new undergraduates who arrived at Trinity with him were cast in a similar mould, essentially products of British upper-class families and the public-school system, including three other boys from Gresham's. Variety was provided by a Siamese Prince, a pair of Americans, two Indians and one young man from West Ham Secondary School in the East End of London. Several of Erskine's contemporaries were the sons of his father's contemporaries whilst the Master, Sir Joseph Thomson the distinguished scientist, would no doubt recall the elder Childers if for no other reason than his much publicised contest for the Magpie and Stump Presidency in 1892.

Ever since he could remember there had never been any doubt but that he would go to Cambridge, a place that had fascinated him since his first visit in February 1922 when the school had been given a day's holiday on the occasion of Princess Mary's marriage to Viscount Lascelles. Then he had gone to Emmanuel and Trinity Colleges, been charmed beyond words by King's College Chapel ('I can't express my love of it') and complained that motor-cycles ruined the atmosphere. Now he was to spend three years there reading for a history degree and clearly relished the prospect, despite the fact that the need to economise in every every way possible had been impressed upon him once he had been denied the opportunity of a scholarship.

Letters which passed between Erskine and Ruth, who was in Ireland, provide first-hand evidence of impressions and reactions during the first days of university life. Only hours after arrival he was writing:

I believe I am the happiest yet loneliest freshman in Cambridge. Already I have an invitation for lunch with the music hostess in Cambridge. I am smoking the pipe it is a beauty. Landlady is a jewel. Yes, I am going to prepare now and am going to fill my mind with knowledge particularly applicable to Ireland and I am going to build up an attitude and approach to life which no mortal can barricade. I expect the same of you.

A quick note the following day largely comprised an S.O.S. for an old mackintosh, suspender garters, an incense-burner (for frying bacon), a bowl and a lamp-shade (buy at Switzers), but a long letter at the week-end was more expansive:

This is a wonderful place. Every stratum of intellectuality and character is to be found. The vast majority of boys from other schools are not unspotted by the world. I mean their eyes and looks show that they have been contaminated with vice if they have not participated in it. There seem to be two types, those who have closed the door against music and those who have not . . . I am joining the cross country running club also University Labour Club which anyone interested in progressive government regardless of private opinion can join.

Then, commenting on Mattins at Holy Trinity Church which he had attended:

The service was inspiring with the limitation that depends on the priest. I think I shall go there often. For he tackles the problem of religion in life seriously and God in His Church comes in diverse ways to help the people. In the R.C. Church one feels it is curative not preventative. It is not up to modern needs, does not face them. In an age when a loosening of the Ne Temere decree is most needed, it is strengthened in severity . . . the finer people in the Protestant (Episcopalian) Churches are expanding, throwing off old fetters. Confession of C of E never impresses me . . . it is too mechanised a piece of thought — expresses too much what can be felt sincerely in a minute and is too extreme and negative.

Erskine's rather cramped rooms were at a tall, terraced house in Chesterton Road, some ten minutes, brisk walk from Trinity College. The front of the house overlooked the River Cam winding its way through Midsummer Common and in the early morning or late evening stillness the sound of the water racing through an adjacent lock could be clearly heard.

Six portraits adorned the walls of Childers's rooms and represented the two major themes in his life. Father, mother and Ruth were his closest personal ties, Eamon de Valera, Liam Lynch and Liam Mellows symbolised his political faith. After only three weeks in Cambridge these strands came together when he slipped across to Dublin for a couple of days to attend his father's burial in the Republican Plot at Glasnevin Cemetery. This was a moving experience that brought back vividly the events of two years before and Erskine drew much comfort from Ruth's presence.

Ruth was currently living with Molly Childers at Bushy Park Road, acting as her companion and busying herself preparing articles for American newspapers on such diverse topics as Indians in London, Dublin beggars and the problems of coloured seamen. Inevitably she was also drawn in to certain secretarial work for Sinn Féin as Molly had recently been elected Joint Treasurer with Mrs Caitlín Brugha, another well-known Republican widow. During the Civil War and its immediate aftermath the Government elected by the Second Dáil still held itself to be the country's legal authority and 'President' de Valera was clinging fast to the structure of Sinn Féin as the best means of ultimately effecting political advance. It was essential that the machinery of the party be kept intact, though, even before his release from prison in August 1924, he had conceded to himself that an abstentionist policy had no long-term future. 'Shadow' cabinet committees were thus still functioning and for a short time Ruth acted as secretary at some of their meetings. Her social-science training was particularly beneficial to the Public Health Advisory Committee. The tremendous contribution made by women to the Republican cause in the years from 1922 to 1925 is frequently overlooked, but it is arguable that without their unselfish devotion when most of the menfolk were in hiding or imprisoned the structure and organisation might have suffered irretrievably.

Back in Cambridge Erskine was taking a close interest in British politics. He had welcomed the advent of the first Labour Government under Ramsay MacDonald as a break in the old pattern and ignored Ruth's warning not to link up with the University Labour Club lest it should prejudice his later work in Ireland. One notable speaker was Saklatvala, already known to Erskine and much respected by him and Ruth. Alas, such respect for the Communist M.P. was not widespread and he was hounded by a hostile mob from the time that he arrived at Cambridge railway station. Smuggled in to the meeting he slept at a 'secret' address before breakfasting with Erskine who took him by borrowed car as far as Newport (Essex) in an effort to ensure an unmolested journey back to London. Another leading speaker was Jimmy Maxton who seems to have made a good impression:

I heard a Clydesider tonight. They have fine things in them the Clydesiders, weaknesses of course and they are ignorant of prejudice in relation to the capitalist menace but he said some fine things. I am more and more a socialist. Private enterprise is useless and wicked, the credit of the country must be nation-alised that is vitally important. If we are to have a stable civilisa-tion the state must start co-operatives and nationalise industry and when they have got it working they can decentralise if the simpler life socialism anticipates, is realised.

Something of the objectivity, if not cynicism, which his mother displayed during World War I is evident in a letter which Erskine wrote to Ruth on Armistice Day 1924 when vast crowds gathered in towns and cities throughout the British Isles to observe the two-minute silence at 11 a.m.

I have just been watching the crowds in the market place. It was interesting to feel the various moods of the people in a silence in which one could hear a pin drop. Two things strike one. The gullibility and obstinacy of the educated and the ignorance of the uneducated people. Each year the armistice feeling becomes less profound as the old world goes on, no better for the sacrifices of the Great War. There were numbers there who stood and believed in Empire, who gloried in war. There was a large number who still believed that their sons and husbands died for freedom and that England still upholds liberty all over the world. There were many disillusioned drawn thither by the herd instinct and to pay respect to the dead more out of custom than with enthusiasm for either Empire or liberty. There were just a few people, men and women with fine faces, poor and rich, who had learned the lesson or were beginning to, like me they came to pay respect to the motives for which most people died in the Great War while remembering with pity the ignorance of mankind ... In the Market Square on the Guildhall were perched hundreds of pigeons. When the guns fired they flew away, a sort of mockery on the unconscious hypocrisy of the crowd.

Left-wing politics in addition to the Gospels were propagated from the pulpit of Thaxted Church and Erskine made several visits to the picturesque Essex village to hear sermons preached by the Rev. Conrad Noel, a controversial Anglican socialist.

The first-year pattern of tutorials consisted of constitutional history on Monday, Wednesday and Friday, economic history on Tuesday and Thursday and Mediaeval history on Tuesday, Thursday and Saturday mornings. Like most freshmen Erskine was inundated with invitations to tea and coffee and it was considered improper to refuse. He attended a debate at the Magpie and Stump to which he was elected a member at the 1177th meeting on 24 October 1924, and spent an enjoyable evening at the Cambridge Musical Club. He told Ruth that his recipe for University life was 'read heaps, write heaps, meet heaps of interesting people and keep fit'. Cross-country running helped to achieve the last objective.

Ruth questioned Erskine's friendship with two older men who lived together and bred Russian wolfhounds, sensing that their relationship was 'unusual'. 'Remember', came the reply, 'that a fellow six feet high a rowing blue, a fine pianist and a fine character who does not intend to marry and who is a terribly close friend of another man who needs him terribly for help is neither immoral or ill and society, I think, is wrong in condemning him as either'. Not long afterwards an incident with homosexual overtones involved a close family friend; it would have been highly embarrassing had it not been treated with deep understanding and in complete confidence.

David Lubbock Robinson had been an unlikely comrade-in-arms of the elder Erskine during his last days. Robinson, who was a relative of Lord Avebury and a grandson of the founder of the Dublin *Daily Express,* spent much of his childhood Delgany in County Wicklow, where his father had been Church of Ireland Rector for some years. Educated in England and at Trinity College, Dublin he qualified as a solicitor and also won several hockey caps for Ireland. During World War I he served with the Royal Marine Artillery, winning a D.S.O., Croix de Guerre and a Mention in Despatches, at the same time losing an eye and suffering severe injuries to his legs. Undaunted, and largely prompted by Robert Barton whom he had known almost all his life, he joined Sinn Féin in January 1919 and by the summer of 1922 was active with the anti-Treaty forces. His cultured accent often caused people to mistake him for Childers senior and the two were arrested together while travelling secretly from Cork to Dublin, Robinson subsequently serving a total of eighteen months' imprisonment.

This tough, courageous man, whose reputation in gaol rested on his equal readiness to help fellow prisoners and abuse the Free State warders, revealed another side of his character to Erskine not long after his release when he was living at Glendalough House assisting Robert Barton to run the estate. Having confided his state of utter loneliness he went further, as Erskine related to Ruth in a letter demonstrating a depth of mature understanding in an age which still affected to look askance at some aspects of human nature:

He needs tenderness and affection. He wants someone to love and devote himself to and Bob is as hard as a rock as you know. Then his voice caught and he looked up and said shyly, 'You know Erskine, I fell in love with you when I came out of prison but I knew you were probably ignorant of what that kind of love means and I couldn't do it. But I am so lonely here.' I was staggered . . . I felt a wave of tenderness, of wishing to heal the wounds of war and his loneliness. But think of him wanting to fall in love with *me* and not doing it out of fear that I wouldn't understand . . . When we left David gave me a strange look of agony in his face, of course, no one knows about him and we must never tell anyone. But it must be fearful for him.

I have come at last to believe that the actual presence of that quality in mens minds is not abnormal. Abnormality is lack of balance in any action. If human love be disproportionate in its different aspects then it is abnormal . . . David is going to be a problem for now he has told me our relations are self consciously felt. I shall have to talk to you about what to do with him. I can try and fill his life, invite him to Cambridge, give him books write to him, get him to tell me his troubles but that itself has its dangers. Loving you gives me such a longing to give him human love and yet I see the difficulties. Oh, darling, isn't life strange. Think of the tragedies caused, the unanswerable opportunities missed through fear of others or through hatred of it. How it explains David, his fascinating analysis of things, his devotion in prison to others, his narrowness in certain things. You must be loving to him. I wish I could help him.

The March 1925 edition of the *Trinity Magazine* featured a light-hearted 'Who's Who' on various undergraduates and included the following entry:

> E. H. Childers . . . A zealot with a mad ideal in reach,
> A poet just about to print his ode.

Certainly poetry was already an essential ingredient in his life and he frequently wore the thoughtful, abstracted look of a poet searching for a vital stanza. The assumption must be that the ideal was re-establishment of an Irish Republic. Yet it is just possible that it was marriage; for an undergraduate to contemplate this happy state in the 1920s (unless honour was at stake!) would be widely held to be akin to madness. After an abnormally eventful school life as a result of his father's actions Erskine now seemed hell-bent on ensuring for himself that his Cambridge years would also be markedly different from those of his contemporaries.

After only a few months' acquaintance, letters to and from Ruth demonstrated the passionate intensity of the love which each had for the other. At Easter 1924 the subject of marriage was first mentioned during a walk in the Wicklow Hills and some sort of understanding was reached.[1] Molly Childers had always welcomed the friend-ship, liked Ruth immensely and believed that her son's infatuation would pass. Mrs Osgood, who was likewise fond of Ruth, had urged on her from the start the necessity that nothing should interfere with her grandson's studies. However, in November 1924 Ruth was writing, 'I believe sometimes that our love has grown past even what Mother believes it to be — that it is growing past even our recognition. Yet we must guard it carefully.'[1] Looked at objectively, marriage presented insuperable difficulties. Erskine was six years younger and though mature far beyond his years was nevertheless still a student and in no position to support a wife. The very idea, according to the conventions of the time, was quite absurd.

Ruth suffered appendicitis in Dublin and her family anxiously pressed her to go home to America for a holiday. Once the requisite fare arrived she could delay no longer. A passage to New York was booked for the end of March prior to which she spent a month touring the north of England and West Midlands garnering material for projected articles on the industrial scene. Erskine went to great efforts planning an itinerary which inevitably finished at Cambridge where Ruth spent several days. They borrowed a car for a few hours and raced over to Holt for tea with J. R. E. at Gresham's School.

By the time that Ruth sailed from Southampton aboard the S.S. *Mauritania* the fateful decision had been taken to marry as soon as possible and the repercussions had commenced. From Paris where she was staying Mrs Osgood wrote at once to Ruth:

You know that I entirely disapprove of your plan to marry Erskine while in college — it has been a terrible blow to me and made me really ill. You know I love you and I have always looked upon you as a wise woman — I could never feel the same if you did this. The woman should be the wise and far seeing one. The man is often impetuous and needs the woman's wise judgment — I have looked forward to being with you and Erskine, looked forward with joy to it. It would never be the same if that occurred — I am almost broken hearted over it, darling — I hope it will never happen.

In a note to Erskine she threatened to withdraw the allowance which enabled him to study at Cambridge, told him he was unfair to his mother, that marriage would wear him out and that the Dean of Harvard suggested such a step would be very foolish.

Fate decreed that angry grandmother and recalcitrant grandson met almost immediately, for he crossed to Paris at the start of the Easter vacation for a visit that by all accounts was one of unrelieved misery. Much of this time was spent arguing with the indomitable, indefatigable, seventy-seven-year old Mrs Osgood. 'Grandmother is so antagonistic to everything I do', Erskine wrote to Ruth; 'she harps on how wonderful Hamilton is (an American cousin), how lovesick I am, how unwise you are, the evils of smoking, how cruel I am to mother, how much she'd do for us if we want, how she'll cut off everything if we don't and how she doesn't wish me to see anything strange in Paris ... till I'm nearly mad!' A few days later, writing from the Pullman express between Dover and Victoria, he was more positive. 'I think we must marry at Cambridge if it's possible. Grandmother says three years from last October, mother says 25 and says she doesn't object to grandmother helping us ... looking back Paris seems like a dream of conflicting, agonising struggle. Yet the fascination of beauty there is in Paris. I wanted not to escape!' In London for a couple of days there was no respite from his grandmother's chiding tongue and one evening Erskine was pleased to escape from the hotel to the sanctuary of a Lyons Corner House!

In Dublin for the remainder of the vacation the marriage controversy rumbled on. Molly was torn between supporting her mother and placating her son, and Erskine found the situation depressing:

Oh, I am feeling so lonely at this minute. I am alone in the study and mother is busy. It is 10 p.m. and a gale blows and the windows shake. This afternoon I have been reading father's letters and missing him, missing things he would give us which no mortal can, missing him with an ache of misery. I feel exhausted with loneliness. Oh, I am so lonely too for you my angel, why does life separate us when I most need you after all that has happened. I have gone through it all terribly too while thinking of father.

Back in Cambridge Erskine announced his intention of devoting the time to work and preparation, but despite such high-mindedness there was some relaxation. An enjoyable Sunday was spent with the Cornford family, where he was directly in touch with the flourishing literary circle that had characterised Cambridge and immortalised the near-by village of Grantchester in the decade prior to the Great War. Francis Cornford was a Classics Don at Trinity College and his wife Frances, a granddaughter of Sir Charles Darwin, was a poet of considerable repute. Twenty years previously she had befriended the undergraduate Rupert Brooke, whom she once described in a sentimental epigram as a golden-haired young Apollo. She was highly complimentary about a poem which Ruth had sent her, also about Ruth herself: 'how lovely she is Erskine and what a life — full of what possibilities ahead of you both.' Something of the feeling of Brooke's best-loved poem seems to have transmitted itself to Erskine as he rested alongside the Cam one warm May evening, waxing lyrical. [2]

I have been sitting close to the river in the moonlight, terribly still. Soft green fields all glitter with dew. There is the scent of spring flowers. In the west a crimson glow in the aftermath of sunset. Heavenly silence is broken only by a nightingale pouring forth its song, the song of joy that knows no sorrow. Tall Lombardy poplars, netting the moon, they seem so ghostly now shimmering green, then grey and mauve in the strange light. To the east utter darkness. Mists cling to the earth and drift across the fields. Here is peace, no harshness of outline, no jarring sounds, only the moon across the sky. After the crowds, the noise and confusion of life in the town it fills the soul with joy. Yet there is a sadness on the scene. The moon is old and a little weary of coldly reflecting the burning sun to the deaf multitudes. I lay on the ground and felt the sweetness of the earth, the joy of spring — and over me there flowed a radiance of light which came not from the moon but from a greater source ... I lay still afraid to spoil the vision.

Another notable Edwardian Cambridge figure made a less than favourable impression on Erskine, who described Professor Maynard Keynes as a 'horrid looking man, not at all a lovable character. He goes in for every form of pleasure except drink.'

In America Ruth was sick for Erskine and for Ireland.

'The whole trouble with this country is that it breeds the philosophy of grab, grab, grab and let me grab more than my neighbour', she wrote and was more expansive to a *Boston Globe* reporter:

What I like about Ireland is that life is simple and real and spiritual there. The Irish people are not so busy making money that they have no time to do what my New England ancestors called 'just settin' and thinkin' '. There are no long lines of motor cars along the roads on Sundays but there is a long line of donkey carts outside the Churches. There are no 'quick lunch counters' every hundred yards but there is a warm Irish welcome, a 'cup of tay and a spud' waiting every wanderer to the thatched cottage doors — all these wonderful old-fashioned qualities are still alive in Ireland. I suppose it is because Ireland has been laid bare of material possessions, even necessities and the Irish people in all their poverty and suffering have turned to the life of the spirit, while we other Nations have been getting rich. [3]

But it was the marriage controversy above all else that dominated. The Dow family were uncertain except for Ruth's brother, Winthrop, who thought the idea was foolish because of the age difference. One of Erskine's American relatives questioned the Dows' social pedigree! The Childers aunts were favourable, Molly continued to waver and eventually Mrs Osgood withdrew her threat to stop the financial support which enabled her grandson to study at Cambridge.

In the University, where married undergraduates were almost unheard of, there was concern that marital responsibilities would detract from work. However, wiser counsels were aware that Childers had missed a stable home background during his adolescence and believed that the help and encouragement of a wife would be a positive benefit and direct his energy and talents to the best effect. A tendency towards exhibitionism and intolerance rather in excess of the natural characteristic of a small man making up for a lack of inches had been perceived by friends who believed that the care of a devoted wife would gently restore any missing inner confidence. [4]

Appropriately in view of their mutual ancestral connection, the marriage of Erskine Hamilton Childers to Ruth Ellen Dow on 26 September 1925 took place in the Congregational Church at Exeter, New Hampshire. A few miles inland from the beaches of Hampton and Rye where Atlantic rollers pound the shore, Exeter is noted for its elm-shaded streets and boys' preparatory school. The wedding provided an occasion for the New England clans to gather at the white-framed Church where the bride had attended Sunday School and the Dow family were regular worshippers. Albert Nelson Dow, a General in the State National Guard, had settled in the town as a young man and made his mark there as a forester and banker. Ruth, his elder daughter, had been educated locally at Robinson Female Seminary before going on to Wellesley College, where her outlook broadened and her intellect flourished. [5]

Despite the absence of the bridegroom's immediate family the spirit of Irish Republicanism was certainly present as David Robinson was the Best Man. Among the wedding-gifts was a book by Thomas Davis, a present from Eamon and Sinéad de Valera, in which one passage had been underlined in red ink:

You who aspire to power must be up and doing. You will, ere you reach the goal, need an amount of labour little thought of when starting. Though disappointment and suffering have somewhat touched you — has it not strengthened you even when it humbled you?

Wedding photographs depict an absurdly youthful-looking bridegroom whose small stature belied even his nineteen years. Molly wrote from Dublin:

Man and wife and my son and daughter. By the time you receive this you will be married and will know the wonderful effect of that Holy ritual, the effect of the satisfaction and self-dedication so solemnly made. There is inspiration in the service which I think no noble creatures can do without ... Do not look at us but whither you are going. You will feel us near you whenever you

57

sit and listen for us. Father and I are there with you, loving and blessing you and knowing and understanding and sharing the divine miracle.

After a honeymoon spent touring the White Mountains in the north of New Hampshire and Vermont the couple sailed from New York back to the reality of the Old World. In Cambridge they took a tiny attic flat above a sanitary engineer's showroom overlooking Sidney Sussex College in the centre of the City. Henceforth Erskine's participation in the usual round of University activities, which make life so worthwhile for the majority of undergraduates, was negligible. After his marriage most close contemporaries hardly saw him and there are no records of appearances in such places as the Union or Magpie and Stump Societies. Coming up to Trinity College in autumn 1925 Mervyn Roberts, a close friend and study companion at Gresham's School, found Erskine very much bound up in domestic bliss and saw relatively little of him.

Doubtless the newly-weds were deeply happy and content with their own company and there was much to do, as Ruth obtained a secretarial job to eke out the meagre finances. But new and old friends were welcomed and entertained. A married undergraduate was novelty enough for the period but a rabid Irish nationalist with an attractive and vivacious American wife was probably unique in the history of the University. Small wonder that rumours were soon circulating to the effect that Childers wasn't working hard enough.

The cynics were confounded when the first part of the Historical Tripos examination was passed with honours but further distraction was in store. By Christmas 1926 Ruth was pregnant and her condition led to Erskine's missing most of the Easter 1927 term, necessitating a further year of study. With the consequent loss of income it was essential that Erskine should find a summer job and he wrote to Carlos Drake, the Chicago hotel and travel magnate to whom he had been introduced by his grandmother. The reply was encouraging:

I was very glad to hear from you. Your willingness to do some courier work this summer interests me greatly. I have a rather pleasant memory of you, coloured slightly by the glamour of those Roman days. Somehow I cannot help feeling you are the kind of individual I should keep in touch with ... so long as your financial condition is not overripe!

Thus, while Ruth went to Dublin for the birth of her daughter, Ruth Ellen, Erskine spent the long vacation acting as a courier for parties of Americans touring England, working directly under Plunkett Fraser, an Irishman who looked after European operations for Carlos Drake.

Back in Cambridge the flat seemed even smaller and was patently unsuited for rearing an infant. But generous help from students and from wives of some of the academic staff enabled all crises to be surmounted and, summoning all the powers of concentration which he had inherited from his father and grandfather, Erskine studied hard enough to pass part II of the Historical Tripos in June 1928 to graduate as a Bachelor of Arts.

So ended an unusual university career. Even during the first year at Trinity College his participation in the wider sphere was inhibited lest any action or utterance should affect his work for Ireland in later years, while the marriage controversy tended to dominate his thoughts for much of the time. Membership of various clubs and societies appears to have been essentially nominal. There seems to have been no especial friend or group of friends and no individual appears to have exercised much influence on his thinking. Later, during his ministerial period, he was to say that he would have preferred to read medicine than any other subject. Yet the experience and privilege of studying at Cambridge was something Erskine Childers treasured for the rest of his life.

Chapter V
A PARISIAN INTERLUDE

During the necessary extra year at Cambridge Childers was spared one nagging worry which afflicts many under-graduates in their final period of study. With future employment already secured he was free to concentrate on work. Ever since schooldays the future had been prob-lematic, for as long as the Irish Free State Government remained in power it was virtually impossible to consider working in Ireland; equally unthinkable was any position under the Imperial Government; to continue in academic life was attractive yet impractical, and opportunities in the United States were discounted as neither Ruth nor Erskine had any desire to move, even temporarily, to the other side of the Atlantic. Once he complained to his mother that 'money is a difficult thing to earn when the British Empire, the Government, the Church, the vested interests and many of the people are against you'. The odds must indeed have appeared to be stacked against him as he speculated on a job in education or local government in Ireland if a Republican Government was established. Molly had replied reassuringly:

In big outline the answer is that like father you will have further years of work which will increase your powers for Ireland. His work reading for the Bar, his years in the House of Commons, his experience in South Africa . . . then the Great War itself . . . all these were so many tools in his hand when he gave himself for Ireland. You start along the road and will carry on from where he left off so far as faith goes, but all that you plan, even the bitter years of exile will increase your powers for Ireland. Every day you will garner experience in dealing with men, in control of men, will learn organisation and all the intricate machinery for getting things done efficiently — above all you will learn to exact discipline.

The highly enjoyable courier work for Drake Travel led to suggestions of something more permanent and in October 1927 Erskine visited Paris to explore the possibilities. After interviews with several commercial and industrial firms he returned in top form. Richer by 1700 fr., approximately £14 stg, which he won playing roulette, he also had two firm offers of employment in his pocket. Carlos Drake's terms of 2000 fr. per month compared most favourably with the 1100 fr. offered by the Bankers' Trust so the immediate future was settled without delay. The concept of a spell away from the British Isles appealed for several reasons, not least for a chance to find an identity outside the sphere where the name Childers was so well known. Crowded, cosmopolitan Paris where both Erskine and Ruth had enjoyed several short sojourns appealed to them enormously.

As soon as examinations finished in June 1928 Erskine left Cambridge for Paris, where a small hotel in the Latin Quarter became his initial base. If the standard was hardly comparable with the luxurious Hotel Regina where he had stayed with his affluent grandmother it was centrally situated not far from the Palais du Luxembourg and the Sorbonne. The student atmosphere of the district was all too familiar. Work commenced in the Drake Offices on Rue Castiglione as Erskine reported enthusiastically:

It is hard to think all day in terms of trains and cars and time-tables. Today I sat in the reception room and attended to people as they came in. The chief difficulty is finding the exact spot in the timetable. I am going to the office after hours to look at all the coupons, books of tickets etc., to get an idea of the system. Carlos is making a lot of money this season. He hints all the time I should replace people in the office who aren't pleasing him.

Coping with the complexities of international travel, the ways of a relatively unknown city, a different language and a dire shortage of cash all taxed the mind of Erskine Childers in the summer of 1928 as he spent most of his spare time pounding the pavements in search of a suitable apartment. But a hint in a letter from Ruth temporarily relegated all other worries to the back of his mind. 'We cannot afford to have two babies' he wrote, as though that would end the matter! But there were compensations. A most satisfactory relationship was established with Carlos Drake, who sent his new Travel Manager off on a wide-ranging tour after only a few weeks. Visiting Versailles and the tourist sights of Paris was tame indeed compared with Switzerland, the Flanders battlefields and a first flight in an aircraft. There was private leisure too, such as the occasion when Robert Childers made a brief stop en route from his Swiss boarding-school and the brothers spent an agreeable evening at the Casino.

By early autumn the Childers family and an Irish nurse were installed in an apartment on Rue Broca not far from Gare d'Austerlitz in a poorer part of the city. After less than six months together Ruth went to Dublin for the birth of her baby and the pull of Ireland and lure of the simple life soon absorbed her thoughts and imagination.

One gets so bound in with worldly things living in Paris that it isn't easy to retire into that inner, inner peace of security where Erskine and I really live with our love and where I especially wanted to be when this baby came. I am here in the imperturbable sanctuary where we wanted so much to be and [nothing] can trouble the equilibrium and poise of spirit that one has.

Successive letters returned to the theme of material, urban prosperity as against the simple, rural life. Following the arrival of the infant, Erskine Barton Childers, Ruth spent a couple of blissful weeks at Glendalough. Then she made it her business to look up as many contacts as possible, enquiring and probing as to likely avenues of employment if de Valera should form a Government, abolish the Oath and re-establish a Republic. Seán O'Uadaigh, Austin Stack, Art O'Connor, Robert Brennan and Jack B. Yeats were among the people who Ruth thought would be useful contacts.

Business boomed at Drake Travel in the spring of 1929 and office pressures prevented Erskine from slipping over to Dublin to see his new-born son. A record number of American tourists were booked for the season, many attending the Spanish-American Exposition in Barcelona and Seville for which the firm acted as official agents. Selling tourism throughout Europe involved meticulous planning of detailed itineraries, virtually all travel then being by land and sea. Arranging barge trips on the Danube, cruises on the Rhine, jaunts further afield to India and the Orient, not to mention safaris in darkest Africa for the richer and more adventurous, were all in a day's work.

More usually there were travel tickets to supply, information to impart or local sightseeing trips to supervise. Drake Travel owned a fleet of Hispano-Suiza limousines, driven by White Russian aristocrats who had fled from their homeland at the time of the Bolshevik Revolution. James Joyce, self-exiled from Ireland, and the film star Gloria Swanson were among the better-known clients. All in all the job provided an outlet for Erskine's administrative ability, bringing variety and contact with numerous facets of Parisian life. English by birth and upbringing, Irish through filial devotion, he was perhaps a Parisian by inclination and temperament. Speaking French like a native he grew to love French culture, as he told the Dáil some forty years later during a debate on E.E.C. membership. [1]

When Ruth arrived back with Ireland tugging at her heartstrings she found her husband busily absorbed and sharing in his firm's prosperity. A Buick motor-car was purchased and the family moved to a larger apartment in the fashionable suburb of Neuilly-sur-Seine, close to the river and the Bois de Boulogne — the large open space on the western side of the city modelled on London's Hyde

Park. 'We are too respectable and comfortable for words', Ruth wrote in a letter to the *Wellesley College Magazine*, summing up her Parisian life with, perhaps, just a touch of exaggeration.

We romance on all that Paris has to offer. We leave cards on wonderful old French families; we take children to see the puppets' shows on the Champs Elysée; we discuss art with a few French and more especially a German artist; we listen to a Jewish composer at work; talk writing with half a dozen cosmopolitan folk, novelists, biographers and newspapermen and play roulette with the younger married Paris-American set. [2]

In the period between the end of the Civil War and the conclusion of the decade, when Erskine Childers was at Cambridge and in Paris, the political scene in Ireland changed quite radically. As the Cumann na Gaedheal Government under President W. T. Cosgrave laid the foundations of the new State, the Republican wing led by de Valera moved rapidly through several phases. The Oath of Allegiance to the British Monarch, enshrined in the 1922 Constitution of the Irish Free State, was anathema to those deputies elected in 1922 and 1923 and prevented them from taking their seats in the Third and Fourth Dáils as the official Parliamentary opposition. Yet by-election results, particularly following the Army mutiny of 1924 and the Boundary Commission fiasco in 1925, indicated a continuing groundswell of support for the Republican ideal.

Once the I.R.A. had broken with Sinn Féin in November 1925 de Valera moved to resolve the dilemma at the Annual Conference (Ard Fheis)*, in March 1926. Defeat on a motion that attendance at the Dáil was a matter of policy rather than principle led to his immediate resignation as President and he quickly began the process of forming a new party. Fianna Fáil (The Republican Party) was formally launched at a rally in La Scala Theatre, Burgh Quay, Dublin on 16 May 1926 with the support of most of the anti-Treaty Sinn Féin deputies and the following objectives:

*Literally means high feast, pronounced 'ard-esh'.

1. To secure the Unity and Independence of Ireland as a Republic.
2. To restore the Irish language as the spoken language of the people, and to develop a distinctive national life in accordance with Irish traditions and ideals.
3. To make the resources and wealth of Ireland subservient to the needs and welfare of all the people of Ireland.
4. To make Ireland as far as possible economically self-contained and self-sufficing.
5. To establish as many families as is practicable on the land.
6. By suitable distribution of power to promote the ruralisation of industries essential to the lives of the people as opposed to their concentration in cities.
7. To carry out the democratic programme of the First Dáil.

Thirteen months after formation Fianna Fáil passed its first electoral test by securing exactly the same number of seats (44) as had the Republican front in 1923. The rump of Sinn Féin succeeded in only five and were obviously a spent force in any meaningful political sense. On 12 August 1927 Fianna Fáil deputies complied with the letter of the contentious Article 17 and took their seats at Leinster House. Public approval of this decisive step came the following month when the party won fifty-seven seats at the second general election in four months to become the official Parliamentary opposition in the Sixth Dáil. Thereafter they were breathing heavily down the neck of the tiring Cosgrave administration, which grappled ever more ineffectively with a multitude of problems and as the thirties approached there was a feeling that change was in the air.

By the time Ruth and the two children left Paris for a holiday in America at the beginning of 1930 the business climate had changed dramatically as a result of the recession in the United States and Europe. In a letter to his wife Erskine observed gloomily that only two clients had visited the Drake offices in three days and firms in France were going bankrupt in numbers. The deteriorating situation concentrated his thoughts on the longer-term future and he seized a chance to have several lengthy discussions with his mother. None of the horrific events of the Civil War touched Eamon de Valera more deeply than the execution of his English colleague and adviser. Through the years he kept in close touch with his widow whose devotion to the Republican cause both before and since her husband's death had been an example to all. Despite her incapacity and recurring bouts of pain Molly remained active on the publicity side of Sinn Féin and in close touch with many of its leading figures.

On her first visit to the French capital for almost twenty years Molly Childers determined to enjoy herself. Her programme included visits to the Comédie-Française, the Folies-Bergères and to the cinema to see Charlie Chaplin in *Gold Rush*. She met Carlos Drake and enjoyed several motor drives with Erskine, obviously revelling in a rare opportunity to have her son to herself. The question of the future was thrashed out at length and Molly departed for Dublin resolved to investigate all possible likely avenues of employment in Ireland.

Deeply in love, Erskine and Ruth were miserable apart. The former had moved into an hotel to be with his mother and remarked that he seemed to be the only celibate young person there. Ruth frequently alluded to Ireland:

We have a new Irish servant just landed from Dublin who is so Republican that she nearly shakes with excitement every time she hears me called Mrs Childers. So good to hear her brogue — she is Kerry, I wish the children could have an Irish accent.

Whilst in America the two children were christened, a telegram reassuring Erskine that the service was 'all arranged simply as I told you, not involving doctrines'.

The remaining fifteen months or so that the Childers family spent together in France was, by and large, a period of worry and uncertainty. A move was made to a less prestigious apartment in Rue de Longchamp whilst Drake Travel cut its losses by moving to smaller offices in Rue de la Paix. A third child and second son, Roderick Winthrop, was born in Paris in June 1931 and as soon as he could travel was taken with his brother and sister to America, the intention being that Erskine should eventually join his family there for a brief holiday. Unfortunately the affairs of Drake took a turn for the worse and all the staff agreed to sacrifice one month's salary. There was only a fifty-fifty chance of the company surviving and Erskine wrote that it was all 'very grim and ghastly and I see little light'. The apartment was given up, furniture stored, and instead of crossing the Atlantic his only break was a quick drive round the south of England with some Canadian friends, visiting favourite haunts such as Bath and the Wiltshire Downs.

As the leaves on the trees in the Bois turned all shades of brown in the autumn of 1931 a solitary young man could often be seen striding the pathways deep in thought. His wife and children were thousands of miles away and had no home of their own; he was short of cash and shortly would have no job. In one letter to Ruth, Erskine sounded almost desperate, 'for God's sake send me four pairs of socks — two greyish blue and two brown'; and one can only speculate whether the financial situation, a shortage of darning wool or even lack of ability with the needle was responsible! There was no shortage of suggestions for the future. Ruth suggested a course at the Harvard Business School and his grandmother too thought that her grandson should undertake further study in America provided Ruth could obtain a job in Boston to help the finances. On reflection Ruth had second thoughts as the following letter reveals:

I long for a peat fire and the smell of peat burning and nothing that counts is in Paris or New York. We must learn Irish, rent a cottage near Glan and if Dev gets in — we can't have both money and Ireland and I consider money as nothing beside Ireland. The question is, will the children? I do not think you want to come here and postpone Ireland for years. I want you back before you are thirty. Then the children will be young enough to have an

Irish upbringing. If they know you have been studying Irish in Paris it will convince everyone you have been preparing all the time you have been away — in other words that you are not a returned Irishman who went away and then came back.

However, it was something in a long letter from Molly Childers, written some time before, that provided a clue as to where the future lay. As she had promised Erskine during her Paris visit she spared no effort in looking into all possibilities and the letter is worth quoting in full.

I started digging up the roots of things as they are and comparing them with possible alternatives. I consulted Dev, Frank Gallagher, Seán O'Uadaigh and Mr Lyon [a solicitor neighbour].

1)   F.F. paper to be out possibly next March. You could get a post on the staff. I am all against you committing yourself to any party policy of such a kind. You might be involved.

2)   Frank G. College lectureship, later professorship. Salary — starvation wages, highest to National University Professors £300 p.a. Trinity better but a Republican debarred.

3 & 4) S. O'Ud. & Mr Lyon. Best prospects in legal profession although it is now flooded with aspirants. Even so, quite feasible from worldly point of view. From political it entails recognising Free State Courts. The reality makes it undesirable. Would entail five years preparation ... Seán says a deeply interesting and moving work that of Solicitor. There remains Ford of Cobh.* You might see Ford in America and try that out. The national question must determine. One must weigh seriously prolonged absence, of course. If you could get work here it would be wise. IF!! Wish Drake would come to Ireland. You might find some go-ahead American firm who would send you here as an agent developing some new industry.

P.S. I feel that Father would long for you to come soon. Would he be S.F. now to the point of moving all possible factors against F.F. .... I know he would be against that — he said to me that he believed were the F.S. to win and function there would be found a way through the Parliamentary machine to win freedom — to 'leak' out of the

*The Ford Motor Company established a factory at Cork in 1932.

Empire without need for further physical force methods
... businessmen believe F.F. will win next time.

And do you know I believe S.F. will act more vigorously
against F.F. if this happens than they are now acting
against the F.S. Government. That is a dreadful thing to
say but that is really the psychology of S.F. now. Terrible
and you in all this (if you came back now I would still want
you out of party politics and I think you feel the same), if
you were here you could do the work needed by acting on
human material — by inspiring youth, by lectures, by re-
organising etc., not as a political candidate or protagonist
in the arena but as a teacher or prophet, as a *trainer*. This,
until the material was ready to be tempered and fashioned
into the kind of tool needed for the future.

The first possibility alluded to, the 'F.F. paper' as Molly
termed it, was for Eamon de Valera a dream about to come
true. One aspect of the national scene which weighed
heavily with him since the Civil War was the fact that all of
the daily press and most local newspapers were against
him. A scheme to take over the *Freeman's Journal* came to
nought and collection of the vast amount of money necessary to start up a new national daily paper, sympathetic to
Republican aims, commenced. A Republican Daily Press
Fund was established in 1926 with Austin Stack as Chairman and Molly herself as Hon. Treasurer.

In September 1931, rather later than once envisaged and
thanks to generous financial help from America, the first
edition of the *Irish Press* rolled off the presses at Burgh
Quay, Dublin. The project had involved many of the
leading Republican figures. Editor Frank Gallagher, an
amiable Corkman, had once been a journalist at Westminster and worked closely with Erskine Childers senior in
production of the 'Irish Bulletin' during the War of
Independence. He brought the paper a breadth of vision
and experience. Within a few weeks of the launching the
bearer of another noted Republican name visited the
offices.

Home from Paris for a few days, Erskine was warmly

welcomed when he went to see Eamon de Valera, who was
well aware of his unshakable commitment to carry forward
his father's work in Ireland. The general political situation
was discussed and it was made clear that Erskine's
presence in the Dáil would be required as soon as the Oath
had been abolished and a suitable seat arose. Meanwhile a
job on the *Irish Press* was available, though the salary
would be minimal. After a further meeting with Frank
Gallagher, who initially wanted him as a night editor,
the position of Assistant Advertisement Manager was
accepted at a salary of 5 guineas a week.

A cable advised Ruth to return for Christmas, whilst a
following letter warned her that life was going to be very
tough and enquired whether her father, General Dow,
might provide an allowance. The domestic details slotted
into place, Robert Barton agreeing to store furniture and
Mrs Osgood to pay for a nurse for the children — the family
would live at Bushy Park Road while seeking a suitable
cottage. Another dream was about to become reality and
Erskine returned to Paris in high good-humour, calling at
Holt to see his old Headmaster and at Cambridge to visit
his brother on the way across England.

It was a gamble to exchange the bright, cosmopolitan
French capital for poor parochial Dublin and Erskine had
momentary misgivings. The sojourn at one of Europe's
great cross-roads had enabled him to find his identity and
stand back from the glare of publicity. As a knowledgeable
and efficient travel agent he had made a name for himself
by his own efforts and at the age of twenty-six was ready to
begin his major task in life. Neither at this or any other time
is there any evidence of resentment that his destiny had
been determined firstly by the path that his father chose to
follow and secondly by a promise given in adolescence
when under great emotional strain. His own words in a
letter to Ruth reveal something of his thoughts and hopes.

It is so wonderful to be going back to Ireland to our real life
together. If only eighty years of labour will help make Ireland

a happier place for people, a small perfected state where no one is too rich and if we can become free of England and of old prejudices and of the sense of inferiority begotten by oppression. There is so much to do it almost overwhelms me.

Chapter VI

IN THE SHADOW OF
THE RIDDLE

Less than ten years after members of the Provisional
Government ensured that the elder Erskine Childers
played no further part in Irish history the majority of those
responsible for the fateful decision were fighting for their
political lives. One, Kevin O'Higgins, whose ruthless
speeches to the Dáil during the Civil War became a byword
and who had declared in 1922 that the country was entitled
'to act on its own institutions of self-preservation' and 'will
see that any people coming in here for adventure will get
it',[1] had fallen victim of an assassin's bullet in July 1927.
Joseph McGrath, Eoin MacNeill and J. J. Walsh had left
politics. There can be little doubt that Childers senior was
sincerely felt by many Free State politicians to be an evil
influence and a barrier to peace, whilst the personal antipathy felt towards him by Arthur Griffith had transmitted
itself to one or two individuals, and others harboured
lingering feelings of guilt that the execution had taken
place while an appeal was pending.

In 1922 the name of Erskine Childers had been widely
discredited. Those who signed the death-warrant probably
hoped it would soon be forgotten in Ireland. If a thought
was spared for the family it might have been assumed that
they would in due course return to England or leave for
America. Yet, by coincidence, at the precise moment that
Messrs Cosgrave, Blythe, Fitzgerald, Mulcahy and others
were defending their records during the preceding decade
in anticipation of a general election, Erskine Childers
junior was quietly settling his family into his mother's

house on the south side of Dublin, pledged like his father before him to dedicate his life to the service of Ireland. The year 1932 which proved the beginning of a new epoch in Irish politics was also the start of a new phase in his own life.

Before January was through the Sixth Dáil had been dissolved and after the ensuing election Fianna Fáil, a party less than six years in existence, assumed power having won 72 of the 153 Dáil seats. On 9 March 1932 Eamon de Valera was elected President of the Executive Council and formed an administration with the support of Labour and the Independent, Mr James Dillon. Still largely regarded by their opponents as revolutionary assassins the Fianna Fáil Government faced an opposition whom they looked upon as ruthless executioners. Mistrust, the legacy of the Civil War, was complete. Indeed, as they entered Leinster House at the commencement of the Seventh Dáil, Mr de Valera and his fellow deputies carried revolvers in their pockets fearing that a coup d'état might be attempted. After sending a message of 'respectful homage and good wishes' to Pope Pius XI the new Government began implementing its election promises. A bill to abolish the Oath was introduced within six weeks and Economic War with Britain was declared when Ireland defaulted on the annuity payments to the British National Debt commissioners which had been agreed by the previous administration. The first budget in May 1932 contained forty-three new duties on imported goods. As the world found out during the Eucharistic Congress the following month top hats and formal dress, too reminiscent of the *ancien régime*, were also out! But this essentially Catholic party of the cloth cap, projecting a frugal, Gaelic, almost classless culture and society and elected primarily by a rural vote, was also, for historic reasons, the party of Erskine Childers.

As the nation faced up to the changes and braced itself for yet more, Childers himself was dealing with more immediate personal matters. A cottage was rented on the

slopes of Three Rock Mountain some seven miles south of
the centre of Dublin and the family moved in at the end of
March 1932. It was a relatively easy twenty-minute drive
into the city, where he was installed at the *Irish Press* offices
on Burgh Quay, getting down to work as Assistant Advertisement Manager with his customary energy and enthusiasm, happy at last to be serving the country and the cause
closest to his heart. Within a few months his boss resigned
and Erskine was promoted to take his place.

With English and much Irish opinion fearful of and
hostile to the advent of a Fianna Fáil Government it was
hardly the most propitious time to be selling advertising
space for a Republican newspaper, but the job proved the
prelude to some pleasant personal experiences. Mention of
his name provoked interest wherever he went, though it
was sometimes not his own or his father's latter-day
activities on which discussion centred. Time and again *The
Riddle of the Sands* broke the ice and provided the talking-
point, it being assumed that Erskine himself was the
author or at least that he had inherited a love for sailing.
Nothing was further from the truth as he had ruefully to
admit on occasions when pressed. In fact his mother
disposed of the *Asgard* in 1926 to an English army officer, so
that the diminutive vessel which brought much-needed
arms into Howth in July 1914 was apparently destined to
be forgotten by an ungrateful Irish nation, whereas the
fictional *Dulcibella* lived on in many memories.

Calling on the Dunlop Rubber Company in London on
one occasion, Erskine had an appointment with the Advertising Manager. On arrival, however, he was amazed to be
ushered in to see the Managing Director, Sir George
Harrod. After a brief introduction Sir George proceeded to
reveal a detailed knowledge of *The Riddle*, discussing the
various characters with great authority and reciting chunks
of the narrative off the cuff. As the unusual meeting
concluded Childers was delighted to be told that, although
Mr de Valera and his politics were of no interest or appeal
whatsoever, the son of the man who had written such

a wonderful book was welcome to the advertising business.[2]

On the political front Erskine was active for Fianna Fáil and worked hard in support of Séamus Moore in Wicklow constituency during the 1933 general-election campaign. Though Robert Barton had retired from public life following his defeat in August 1923, the seat was still regarded with special affection by the family and Childers cherished hopes of becoming a Wicklow deputy in due course. He had first been mentioned as a likely Dáil candidate in connection with a pending by-election in County Dublin at the end of 1932.[3] Speaking engagements began to form a part of life's pattern, one of the first being an address 'P.H. Pearse and the Future of Ireland' at the Theatre Royal, Waterford on Easter Sunday 1933. However, as so often, his position was unusual. Whilst grass-roots contact with the party barely existed he was well known to most influential national leaders and was soon a member of the National Executive Committee.

But if Erskine was happily absorbed in his work, the Irish dream of rural simplicity rapidly turned sour for Ruth. The practicality of domestic life in a mountain cottage was far from idyllic except on dry, warm summer evenings when it was possible to sit outside and absorb the view across Dublin Bay. There was no electricity, no drainage, and access was by an unmade track. When a fire was lit the family was virtually smoked out. For much of the time the ground outside was a sea of mud and with three youngsters, the eldest at school, it was a patently unsuitable residence and location. When he was at home Erskine was sometimes lost in thought and rather uncommunicative so that an unsettled and disgruntled Ruth departed for America with the children in June 1933, the only consolation being the fact that she would return to live in a suburban villa in Rathgar.

During the long hot summer of 1933 Erskine slaved away redecorating and furnishing the future family home with much else on his mind. 'I feel terribly restless about

Ireland,' he wrote, 'worried about Fianna Fáil and the lack of propaganda. I must get away and forget everything to do with work and politics otherwise I shall lose enthusiasm. I am seeing Dev on Monday.' Ruth's letters during the three months apart were noticeably more affectionate:

I love and adore you. I hope I shall be nicer to you. I've learned a lot this summer and thought more and settled a great deal of the philosophy of living and of marriage in my mind. It only remains to put it into practice.

But Robert Brennan refused a request for a holiday and Erskine had no respite from politics or personal financial worries, which became so acute he even suggested to Ruth that she should stay away for three weeks longer to save more money.

The spacious red-brick house in Highfield Road, Rathgar with its shady, walled garden soon proved infinitely more suited to the needs of a growing family than the Paris apartment or the mountainside cottage, but suburbia seemed depressingly staid and sedate at first. A cross-section of the Rathgar neighbours included some of the pillars of Dublin's professional and commercial life, hard-working, industrious folk, little affected by the dramatic changes on the national scene. Many had been educated in England and were overtly West British. The erstwhile Westminster constituency of Rathmines, which included Rathgar, had staunchly returned a Unionist MP right down to 1922 and now largely supported the Cosgrave party, believing it to stand for retention of the link with Crown and Empire. But the Protestants were a shrinking sector of the population as many of the younger generation had perished during the War fighting with the British forces, while others were emigrating across the Channel, fearful of the future under Fianna Fáil. Politically there was no common ground with them. In ex-Unionist circles names like Childers and Barton were still tainted with having 'gone over to the other side'.

In many respects settling down in Ireland was far from

easy. Neither Erskine or Ruth had any true Irish roots nor any real link with the Irish people. Both had been educated overseas and there was no residue of school or college friends with whom to renew contact. Initially their acquaintances were largely confined to friends and associates of Erskine's parents. In a sense they were immigrants. But unlike the vast majority of immigrants whose background is left behind in another land and who gradually gain acceptance for what they are themselves, once the secret of their surname was revealed others could immediately slot them into context. It is always difficult for the offspring of a famous or infamous parent to live in the shadow and many flee to the farthest corners of the globe to attain a measure of anonymity. Yet Erskine Childers with his highly distinctive and recognisable name deliberately chose to live in the same corner of the same city as had his father.

Nor were problems confined simply to such things as adjustment, prejudice or the environment. There could be tensions periodically within the family. Molly and her elderly mother still resided in Bushy Park Road, a few minutes' walk away from Highfield Road. Three generations of determined, purposeful American ladies were thus on hand to ensure that Erskine lived up to the considerable amount expected of him. In her late eighties Mrs Osgood was as mentally alert as most women half her age, finally completing and publishing her anthology, *City without Walls*, in 1932. She kept a watchful eye on her grandson. Any hint of deviation from the chosen path would have brought a powerful reminder from his mother as to who he was and of his promise to serve Ireland for the sake of his father's memory. Ruth herself possessed a strong will and tried to dominate the marriage more as time passed. Money was never over-plentiful and her taste in clothes and household goods was on the expensive side. She was ambitious, too, to develop her own career as a writer and in the sphere of social service. They both enjoyed good food and wine whilst Erskine had a penchant for fast expensive cars.

At times the variety and anonymity of Paris or London

must have beckoned invitingly. But Erskine displayed a tenacity which was to characterise his later life and fought hard for acceptance on all fronts. Besides, there were compensations even in the very early days. Not least of these was proximity to Glendalough and the Wicklow Hills. The wellspring of the Childers's Irishness was visited frequently and Erskine could share with his own children the sights which twenty years or so before his father had delighted in showing him. From an early age the youngsters learned to revere the memory of the grandfather they never knew.

With a plentiful supply of living-in domestic help obtainable for wages of under £1 per week social life was not restricted. From Rathgar to the city centre was less than twenty minutes on the No. 15 tram and quicker by car. Possibly on the surface Dublin was a dull place in the thirties compared with other European capitals. But an embryonic diplomatic corps was introducing a new dimension and Ruth had contacts in the American Legation. The theatrical scene was enlivened by the English-born Hilton Edwards and Micheál MacLiammóir at the 'Gate', who like Seamus Kelly, or 'Quidnunc' as readers of the *Irish Times* later knew him, became regular guests at the Childerses' dinner-table. Dinner-parties tended to have a distinctly artistic rather than political flavour.

Open-air recreation was enthusiastically advocated and actively pursued. Erskine frequently cycled in to his office, and they both seized every opportunity to head for the west or south-west for longer breaks. In this way much of the country was explored in depth for the first time. Climbing the hills of Donegal or Kerry proved one of the best ways of escaping from workaday urban pressures, and at his instigation 'Open Air Supplements' were published in the *Irish Press* for several consecutive years, the first on 7 April 1933. These extolled the virtues of cycling and hiking as well as giving a useful boost to youth hostelling.

The Irish Youth Hostels Association (An Óige) had been founded by a handful of enthusiasts in April 1931 and within a few years several hostels opened in County Wicklow and more far-flung parts. Ruth took a keen interest in its activities and was elected to the Publicity Committee in 1934, attending the Fourth International Youth Hostel Conference in Poland the following year.[4] Erskine had a well-trained eye for each and every way in which to promote travel and believed that if young people had an opportunity to visit Ireland at reasonable cost they would see for themselves the magic and beauty of Europe's most westerly island and, hopefully, return home with a different impression to that of political and economic instability conveyed by the newspapers. Equally the youth of Ireland would be able to discover remoter corners of their own land and travel abroad cheaply by means of reciprocal arrangements with other Y.H. associations.

But more weighty matters than youth hostelling normally preoccupied Erskine, who took the keenest possible interest in the progress of the Fianna Fáil Government, especially in the sphere of industry. Professor Joseph Lee of University College, Cork has highlighted the almost hit-or-miss pioneering necessary when Industry and Commerce established its effective independence from the Department of Finance in 1932.[5] The remarkable partnership of Seán Lemass, at thirty-two the youngest member of the Cabinet, and John Leydon, the Permanent Secretary, had very little on which to base decisions and projections. Much of the available statistical information was irrelevant and there was a dearth of crucial data concerning the key variables in the Irish economy. Civil servants received little help from academic economists, who were few in number in the thirties and even fewer had any sympathy with Government policies. Many vital decisions were thus taken more or less on the basis of guesswork and instinct.

Yet, despite all the handicaps, Ireland was beginning a period of economic growth. Industrial employment increased from 111,000 in 1931 to 154,000 in 1936 and 166,000 in 1938, the number of jobs being sharply boosted as a result of the protectionist policy necessitated by the economic war with Britain. Behind sweeping protective barriers Irish-owned manufacturing firms employing Irish labour and using Irish materials whenever possible sprang up all over the country. Formed in 1933 the state-sponsored Industrial Credit Company was helping to finance the upsurge, encouraging new factories to locate away from the Dublin area whenever possible.

But if the Irish Government was ill-supplied with background statistical and marketing information, the same applied in greater measure to industry itself. A few pioneer organisations existed to publicise Irish goods and supply data and back-up, though these suffered from lack of funds and facilities, and industry was often neglected as a consequence of concentration on agriculture. The latter had been well served by the Irish Agricultural Organisation Society, nerve-centre of the co-operative movement, founded by Sir Horace Plunkett in 1894, which led directly to formation of the Department of Agriculture and Technical Instruction in Dublin in 1899. In 1905, best remembered as the year in which the Sinn Féin movement started, the National Agricultural and Industrial Development Association was formed by voluntary members with the object of promoting Irish agriculture, industry and commerce. Arthur Griffith himself expressed the guiding sentiments:

To bring about the unity of material interests which produce national strength, to convince the manufacturer that every improvement in agriculture will increase his home market, and the agriculturalist that every extension of the manufacturing industry will promote his welfare. To convince both that there can be no permanent prosperity for either unless the Nation as a whole is prosperous.

In its early years the National Agricultural and Industrial Development Association produced a buyers' guide and a list of Irish-made articles was circulated. Contacts were made with continental markets and displays of Irish products were arranged in the Dublin office window of the *Irish Homestead* magazine, which was the journal of the IAOS edited by George Russell (AE) from 1906 until its demise in 1923. Unnecessary imports were checked and after World War I, with the upsurge of national feeling, buyers' guides were sent out in thousands to every town and village keen to start a new industry. Mr de Valera opened a permanent exhibition of Irish goods in December 1921, but it was not until the Fianna Fáil Government initiated its policy of tariffs in 1932 that the principal objective of the Association was attained and a National Economic Council was called for. [6]

At the *Irish Press* Erskine Childers had been very much concerned with a 'Buy Irish' campaign which culminated in a competition and special features in the newspaper during April 1933. This had involved liaison with NAIDA and as a result of these contacts the secretaryship of the Association was offered to him in April 1935. Clearly it was a challenging position, offering an opportunity for more direct service to the nation, and with his penetrating mind, capacity for facts and figures and retentive memory, one to which Erskine was ideally suited.

Visiting Ireland in 1938 to write about aspects of national life including the expansion of industry, Austen Lake of the *Boston Evening American* called at the NAIDA offices on St Stephen's Green in Dublin. His report, which referred to Childers as the Director, described him as 'a waterfall of industrial data', surrounded by files of printed reference material, surveys, graphs and statistical information. He, apparently, wore a 'singular expression of intense, half worried purpose', whilst his pride and enthusiasm for what industry had achieved shines through in the interview. The opinion that its potential was so great that it would soon be challenging the supremacy of agriculture is likely to have found more favour with Lemass than with de Valera. Whereas the former viewed industrialisation as the long-term solution to emigration, this conflicted with the latter's dreams of rural self-sufficiency. The reality of the Irish economy had revolutionised Erskine's thinking in the years since 1924, when he had written that he would fight to the last tooth against industrialisation.

Despite some industrial progress certain unpalatable facts soon became obvious. Not least was a national mentality which naturally suspected that Irish-made goods were inferior to English products. Perhaps it was understandable that an emerging country, for so long dependent upon another, should display overt signs of a lack of confidence in itself. Inexcusable was the fact that local authorities placing orders for large quantities of manufactured articles appeared to ignore home products and continued to purchase from the traditional English market. Financing posed problems too. Individuals displayed a reluctance to invest in Irish firms with British stocks promising a better return on capital. Also no State guarantees were then available during the embryonic years of a newly established business so that the individual promoter was frequently obliged to pledge personal credit in order to struggle through. Productivity tended to be on the low side in most instances. Small wonder Childers observed that the spirit of nationality was superficial and mystical in character when it came to supporting the nation in practical terms. Sensitive as he was to human frailty and tolerant towards personal weakness, his patience with what he saw as collective neglect, prejudice or stupidity was not so elastic.

If Erskine was impatient, even exasperated, with certain aspects of Irish life, his wife had been appalled to discover that social welfare was almost non-existent. Charities and religious orders struggled to provide care for the impoverished, but an absence of such things as nursery schools, public playgrounds and welfare workers in hospitals and factories called for action and Ruth strove hard to remedy the situation. As her own children started school she found herself with spare time and attended a welfare course in England. Back in Dublin she was instrumental in forming the first School of Social Service which met at Trinity

College and which trained students to become case workers, hospital almoners and factory welfare workers. In addition she supervised the creation of a nursery school and campaigned for Dublin Corporation to appoint a Director of Welfare and Recreation. Arrival of twin daughters, Carainn and Margaret, in November 1937 curbed some of the outside pursuits for a while and Ruth settled down to further her literary aspirations.

Erskine Childers was beginning to revel in life in Ireland. From boyhood he had devoured the contents of dozens of books on both Irish and European history. Since 1932 he had explored most parts of Ireland and now possessed a detailed grasp of the economy, overcoming for the most part the lack of an Irish upbringing. Contacts in high places in the Fianna Fáil party meant that papers and memoranda which he submitted to various members of the Government on topics such as housing, export bounties and wheat production received serious consideration. Through his influence Seán Lemass attended the Annual Dinner of NAIDA in January 1937, though from their first acquaintance the practical and pragmatic Minister for Industry and Commerce seems to have regarded Childers personally with some reserve.

There was still one thing missing, but the keenly anticipated opportunity to enter public life came finally in the wake of more constitutional changes and a further move towards normalising relationships with the neighbouring island.

Much more than the economic war with Britain had beset the Fianna Fáil Government as the decade progressed. The blueshirt movement under the enigmatic General O'Duffy was firmly quashed after a fresh mandate had been obtained from the electorate in January 1933, and the I.R.A. was declared an unlawful organisation in June 1936 following a series of revolting incidents. As the Crown was further unscrewed from the Harp the controversial Oath disappeared in May 1933; the office of Governor-General was reduced to a joke before disappearing; and the Free

State Senate, regarded by the Government and supporters as Unionist in tone, was abolished in May 1936. The abdication crisis of December 1936 provided an opportunity to remove the King from the Constitution and introduce a novel formula acknowledging the British Monarch as being in a position of 'external association' whenever Ireland was acting with other Commonwealth members.

Clearly the need for a new Constitution had become imperative. De Valera personally devoted an enormous amount of time and thought to this, drafting much of it himself. A President was proposed as Head of State; the Prime Minister retitled An Taoiseach rather than President of the Executive Council; and to widespread surprise a second chamber of the Oireachtas (Parliament) was reintroduced, to be known as the Seanad. Controversy lay principally in Articles 2 and 3, which claimed the whole island of Ireland as national territory whilst accepting that the area to be administered temporarily excluded the Six Counties. Article 44, though a watered-down version of de Valera's original concept which, according to Gerald Boland, would have given the Roman Catholic Church a dominant position in Irish society,[7] formally acknowledged the special position in the State of that Church. The Constitution was approved by the Dáil on 14 June 1937, was endorsed by the electorate (including Mr and Mrs Erskine Childers) in a referendum held concurrently with a general election of 1 July and came into force on 29 December 1937.

The Seanad would consist of sixty senators comprising 43 elected members, 6 university representatives and 11 nominees of the Taoiseach, irreverently dubbed 'Dev's cricket team'. It was originally intended to have a vocational character, and in his professional capacity Childers was an obvious choice. Several days after his name was submitted, however, a rude shock was forthcoming. The Chief Returning Officer advised the Government's Legal Adviser that the nomination was invalid, because Childers was not an Irish citizen and so he was ineligible to stand.

For as long as he could remember Childers had regarded himself as Irish, believing this to be his legal right and entitlement. In his speech before the Military Court and in the statement written days before his execution in November 1922, his father claimed Irish citizenship by virtue of his Wicklow-born mother, Anna Barton of Glendalough House. At the time he failed to appreciate that in order to qualify he would have to be alive on 6 December 1922, when the Free State was to be formally established. His son was thus embarrassed and frustrated by a technicality. Happily the indignity of applying for naturalisation through the normal channels was unnecessary as the Nationality and Citizenship Act passed by Fianna Fáil in 1935 incorporated a provision enabling the Government to give immediately the status of natural-born citizenship to a person, or to the wife or son or daughter of a person, who had rendered distinguished service to the Irish nation. By this means Erskine Hamilton Childers was declared an Irish citizen on 2 March 1938 and duly received the appropriate Certificate of Naturalisation. But the matter was to remain a source of controversy throughout his life and he was constantly called upon to justify his position.

In the late winter and early spring of 1938 other matters occupied the attention of de Valera and his Government. Negotiations with the British Government lasting from late January until the end of April resulted in the Anglo-Irish Agreement ending the economic war and restoring the Treaty ports to Irish sovereignty. With dark clouds gathering on the international scene Ireland was thus enabled to opt for neutrality in the event of conflict. At home Dr Douglas Hyde (An Craoibhín Aoibhínn), scholar, poet, folklorist and a founder of the Gaelic League, a man in whom many threads of Irish life were fused, after agreement by all parties became the first President, an inspired choice that stemmed much criticism of the constitutional change itself. With his prestige and popularity at an all-time high de Valera called another general election in June

1938 after the Government had been defeated on the issue of a Civil Service pay claim. Following an unsatisfactory stalemate result in 1937 he now threatened to abolish proportional representation unless a working majority was obtained.

The suddenness of the decision caught some constituencies by surprise. One such was Athlone–Longford, a newly formed three-member seat previously part of the five-seat Longford–Westmeath constituency. The boundary revision in 1936 created smaller constituencies to make it more difficult for minority interests to gain representation. A third Fianna Fáil candidate or running mate was sought to support the two sitting F.F. members. Locally there was some disagreement and Headquarters intervened. Nobody was more surprised than Childers when he was approached to stand for the large rural constituency, almost in the centre of the country, which included the southern portion of County Roscommon in addition to the whole of County Longford and a part of County Westmeath. His sights had always been set on Wicklow or possibly an urban Dublin seat but no opportunity could be missed and whatever the outcome valuable experience would be gained.

Erskine Childers's knowledge of the constituency he was about to contest was largely superficial. He had driven through periodically en route to the west or north-west and in November 1936 he had visited Longford and met Fianna Fáil deputy James Victory at a meeting to form a branch of the Irish Industrial Development Association. In general, however, the widely spread villages and hamlets were unfamiliar, as were the problems of the small Midlands farmers and traders who formed a majority of the local populace. On the face of it Childers was a strange choice. A background of London, Cambridge, Paris and Dublin hardly blended with the predominantly rural scene and he had no local associations.

An encouraging precedent had been set by Frank MacDermot, who scored an unexpected victory as an

Independent in neighbouring Roscommon in 1932, backed only by farmers and a local ratepayers association. MacDermot's roots lay at Coolavin just across the boundary in County Sligo but he was educated at Downside and Oxford and had spent much of his life in England. Active in Liberal Party circles in London prior to 1914 he served with distinction in World War I as a British Army Major and had subsequently married an American lady. After holding his Roscommon seat in 1933 he formed the short-lived National Centre Party with James Dillon.

Firmly entrenched in the Longford seat was the 'Blacksmith of Ballinalee', Major-General Seán MacEoin. First returned as Sinn Féin M.P. twenty years before, he became one of Michael Collins's most trusted aides in the Civil War and departed from the political arena from 1923 to 1929 to become Chief of Staff in the newly formed National Army. Since 1932 he had represented his home constituency in Dáil Eireann in the Cumann na Gaedheal/Fine Gael interest. Living still in Ballinalee, with a wife from Killashee, he headed the poll in 1937 and looked invincible. The two retiring Fianna Fáil deputies, James Victory and Matthew Davies, were reselected at a convention at Ballymahon before Childers's name was approved and the result appeared to be a foregone conclusion.

Childers entered the campaign belatedly. An after-Mass meeting at Carrickedmond was probably typical. Following an introduction by a Longford County Councillor, Michael Drum, who outlined the candidate's pedigree and credentials, Erskine addressed the gathering. 'I feel shy coming and asking for your votes as a man from the city', he began, 'but I want to tell you I am not a city man. I am from Wicklow and my people are country people ... I understand country problems.' The rest of the speech was devoted to a resumé of his association with the Fianna Fáil party and of the Government's achievements, including comparisons with economic performances in Denmark, Holland and Sweden.[8] The quiet sincerity, innate courtesy, intellectual approach and obvious integrity plus the mystique of the name seemed to compensate for lack of local knowledge, and the style contrasted sharply with the more typical back-slapping, drink-buying, robust rural campaigning. Athlone seemed to be the weakest area and was the scene of a concentrated effort just before polling-day.

When the results were announced de Valera had achieved the desired effect nationally and there was a surprise in Athlone–Longford. At the first count MacEoin headed the poll with 6936 first preference votes, Victory was second with 6107 and Childers third with 4885, over 450 more than Davies. After elimination of the Labour candidate MacEoin was elected at the second count, Davies fell by the wayside at the third and both Victory and Childers clinched it at the fourth. For the latter it represented the first major step in his avowed intention to enter Irish political life and carry forward the work of a beloved father. Two letters among the many received by the new deputy gave him especial pleasure. From Glasson in County Westmeath a constituent, Matt Mulhall, wrote:

The fact that you were elected is all the more gratifying because most of the official people were either [for] Victory or Davies in preference to you. I personally will always be proud of the fact I did all I could to start what I am convinced is going to be a most brilliant career and may God bless and protect you and yours.

From Brook's Hospital, Brookline, Massachusetts where she was recovering from an operation, Molly Childers wrote to her son:

Last night I lay thinking of your future and all it can mean to Ireland to have your giving of fine work and your intelligence and scrupulous dealing used in her service. I say 'your future', it seems to be father's and mine and all our high expectations for you are intertwined.

Chapter VII
ASCENDING THE POLITICAL LADDER

In 1938 Fianna Fáil had been the ruling party for over six years with a front bench comprising men whose qualities and ability were tried and tested, so that rapid promotion appeared unlikely for even the ablest newcomer. Relations with Britain were entering a new phase with one major area of contention — partition — remaining to be resolved. On the international scene ominous clouds were gathering which threatened once more to engulf Europe in a major conflict and these inter-related issues absorbed an increasing amount of Government time and attention.

Irish tails were up following the handing back of the ports which had remained under British sovereignty under a clause of the Treaty. Seán T. O'Kelly said that the British had been whipped at the negotiations. It was naïvely thought that one big political and diplomatic push might resolve partition. Erskine Childers made several propaganda sorties to the North, an area he had previously neglected, in an endeavour to sustain the minority and (perhaps) win the hearts and minds of the Unionists. At Newry Town Hall in October 1938 after a ritual declaration that Ireland was an island of unity with no geographical or racial boundary within its shores he said that an artificial boundary had been created by religious prejudice, forecasting that the children of Orange Lodge members would laugh at their parents in the next generation. But at Newtownbutler, Co. Fermanagh, the next month he caused a few wry smiles himself when he was escorted to the R.U.C. Barracks on arrival.

Rumour quickly spread of his arrest, though the problem was nothing more sinister than a technical difficulty over a Six County road-traffic insurance certificate. Childers addressed the inaugural meeting of the Anti-Partition League at Picton Hall, Liverpool in December 1938 and at Athlone a few weeks later, sharing a platform with Cahir Healy the Stormont Nationalist M.P., he announced an extension of the campaign to South Africa and the U.S.A.[1] But the first I.R.A. bombs in England destroyed any hopes of success and partition remained to provide the justification for de Valera's evolving neutrality policy.

The wider European scene, studied with such care, had concerned Childers for some time. At Kilkenny Town Hall in 1937 he spoke about dictatorships in unequivocal terms:

When people yield their absolute obedience to one man, when they all but deify him, when they have no immediate free democratic control of Government, when they cannot be taught by religious communities, when they set up their State as their God and are kept away from a direct control of its activities, that is godless, un-Christian Government. Russia is only one of several countries proclaiming that system of Government.

In November 1938, supporting a motion 'That this House has Confidence in Mr Chamberlain's Foreign Policy' at Trinity's College Historical Society, he denounced Nazism declaring *Mein Kampf* to be detestable, whilst at Ballyforan in February 1939 he warned of the danger of air attacks from Germany and northern Spain on the east and south coasts of Ireland. Privately his wholehearted sympathy lay with Britain and her allies yet he understood and supported the policy of Irish neutrality, and ceased to comment publicly on the Nazi regimes.

But the broad subject of industry, economics and associated facets of Irish life which absorbed Childers in a professional capacity dominated his thinking at this period and almost invariably brought a contribution from him whenever it was debated in the Dáil. Indeed, the Tenth

Dáil was only six days old when he rose from the back benches on 6 July 1938 during a debate on the Industry and Commerce estimates.

I understood that we are discussing estimates for the Department of Industry and Commerce and it occurs to me to point out to deputies on the opposite benches that of all the estimates this is really the most modest. In 1929 the total was approximately £102,000. This year it is £542,000. I suggest that increase, in view of what has been achieved by the Department, is a very modest one. If the Minister had come and asked for £1M more in order to enable him to bring about genuine industrial development in this country I would have said that it was an amount well worth spending in order to end a position that was started by the former administration.

In this, his maiden speech, Childers proceeded to point out that it was Fianna Fáil rather than Fine Gael which had followed the industrial policy laid down by Arthur Griffith at the Rotunda in 1905, remarking that it was the path of tariff protection which Griffith advocated in his book *The Resurrection of Hungary*. Challenging deputies to study Denmark or Holland or other agricultural nations he said the mentality of the Irish people had lacked national spirit until Fianna Fáil took over and established 300 factories in contrast to the 117 closed by the previous administration.[2]

From time immemorial English minds, including those highly trained and broadly in sympathy with Ireland, have been baffled by a wayward ambivalence in Irish thought and action. Erskine's knowledge of the history, geography, culture and economics of Ireland was greater than that of most native-born Irish people, yet after a decade of living and working among them he was still impatient and mystified by quirks of personal and national life. No text-book could explain the unpredictable workings of the collective or singular mind.

It was impossible to reconcile expressions of nationalistic fervour and patriotic flag-waving with a lack of desire to provide a base from which to aim for economic independence. Irishmen seemed to be absorbed in Anglo-American culture and isolationists at one and the same time. In the Dáil the feelings both of fear of and dependence upon England were difficult to reconcile.

Further evidence of limited Irish horizons and lack of national self-confidence became apparent after Erskine's appointment as Secretary of the Federation of Irish Manufacturers in February 1939. The organisation had been formed in 1932 as the Federation of Saorstát Industries to 'unite the different manufacturers' interests into one Federation where their views can be gathered together for presentation in whatever direction is considered advisable for the advancement of Irish industry'. Originally members were exclusively in manufacturing but the spectrum later broadened to include non-manufacturing industry and the body eventually mushroomed into the Confederation of Irish Industry in March 1970. In direct contact with the everyday problems of those endeavouring to export, Childers became aware of the dire need for some sort of advisory panel that would indicate where to break into overseas markets and would supply relevant information. Clearly an export board was essential if ever Ireland was to break out of its rut of dependence on U.K. markets.

Many of Erskine Childers's early Dáil speeches were not of the type associated with a younger deputy keen to make a name for himself. The Fianna Fáil record was always compared favourably to that of the previous administration, but there was an element of objectivity that was lacking among men who had been shooting each other less than twenty years before. Sometimes he prefaced a speech by saying that he was speaking aside from party prejudice, and occasional appreciation was voiced of his efforts to break down Civil War attitudes. The Tánaiste, Seán T. O'Kelly, once commended his defence of emigration statistics, but Seán Lemass must have winced when Childers suggested that the Department of Industry should be reorganised and more studious planning undertaken during the succeeding five years,.

A background of English public school and Cambridge inevitably set Erskine apart from his seventy-six fellow deputies on the Fianna Fáil benches, with whom he had little in common except a mental scar from the Civil War, support for the Government and the business of the day. He was the sole Protestant on the Government side and certainly the only deputy descended from an English monarch and belonging to a family which once owned vast acres of Yorkshire and the Cambridgeshire fenlands. His whole image and approach was more in keeping with the Palace of Westminster than Leinster House. His position, as a non-Irish speaker in a party dedicated to the restoration of the Gaelic language as the natural tongue of the people, was anomalous, to say the least. It was even impossible to find an Irish form for his name.

The first official language, as Irish became under the 1937 Constitution, was the subject of disagreement between Erskine and his mother. Molly felt that it was prudent for an aspiring politician to be fluent in Irish and several times urged her son to start learning it, pointing out that it was the only missing weapon in his armoury. He disagreed, believing that he would be open to a charge of trying to appear something he was not, and was convinced that he would be better to remain consistent with his expected character. Terence de Vere White has written that the Irish people like unapproachable leaders, much preferring the British Ambassador to look like an English aristocrat rather than find him a back-slapping, golf-club friend to all.[3]

Dedicated to serving Ireland, Childers was, nevertheless, proud of his English family and education, and being a Cambridge man always meant something special. To pretend otherwise was less than honest and he wanted no part of it. There is no evidence that de Valera or anyone else ever hinted that a knowledge of the Irish language would enhance his prospects or that a lack of it would be detrimental.

In addition to a full-time job and duties as a Dáil deputy constituency affairs took time and received his assiduous attention. The majority of country deputies were (and still are) local men who lived in their constituencies and travelled to Dublin for mid-week Dáil sittings. It was relatively easy for them to keep abreast of day-to-day happenings through family and friends and in most cases they had deep knowledge of, or feel for, the area they represented. Childers initially knew relatively few people, little of their problems, and certainly lacked the 'feel' of a native. Furthermore, he was faced with a daunting haul of anything up to 90 miles to attend appointments, meetings or functions in Athlone–Longford. Clearly this was a disadvantage and the mystique of his name would be worthless if he became known as an absentee deputy. Week-end visits were arranged at least once a month and had top priority, though this owed as much to a sense of public service inherited from his parents as to political expediency.

No problems arose while a car was available but once petrol was in short supply after the outbreak of World War II travelling became increasingly difficult. Bus services were drastically reduced and long-distance trains were few and far between owing to shortage of coal for the steam locomotives. On most principal routes the one or two daily trains were slow in the extreme, calling at every station and halt en route. In the early 'forties Erskine Childers was often seen early on a Saturday morning loading his bicycle on to a train at Dublin's Westland Row Station before commencing a laborious journey to the Midlands. The saddlebag contained food, toothbrush and pyjamas, and a briefcase strapped to the crossbar contained letters, notes for speeches and other political paraphernalia.

Typical, perhaps, was the week-end of 30–31 March 1941. Childers arrived at Longford aboard the morning train from Dublin and after lunch cycled to Kenagh to inspect the local tillage campaign. Later he rode on via Ballymahon to Athlone, spending the night at a supporter's house. After addressing several after-Mass meetings on Sunday morning he rode to Clonown to view drainage work on the Hughes Estate and issue an appeal to local farmers to increase tillage. Staying overnight with another constituent, he cycled away at the crack of dawn to Moate to catch the morning train back to Dublin so that by early afternoon he was in the office dealing with a pile of paperwork.[4] Emphasis on personal fitness and a genuine fondness for pedal power were priceless assets and Erskine must have reflected that rides in East Anglia years before were, unwittingly, all part of the training for work in Ireland.

Learning of the visits, the Earl of Granard invited him to stay at Castle Forbes when in the north of the constituency, but the first occasion proved disastrous. After cycling up the drive a hot and tired Erskine dismounted and rang the front doorbell. As the butler was regarding the dishevelled visitor with some suspicion both men were increasingly aware of an all-pervading aroma. The cause was a fish that a constituent had presented earlier in the day and which had been stuffed into the saddlebag. Suggestions that the kitchen entrance might be more appropriate on future occasions were met with amusement and understanding.

Even in baggy week-end tweeds Erskine was every inch a man of cities as he traversed the lanes of Longford and Westmeath during frequent visits. Much of Goldsmith country was undrained and remote, narrow roads winding midst lake and bog through sleepy villages and hamlets with the quietly flowing Shannon to the west of the brooding landscape. There was a timelessness about Clonbroney, Curraghboy, Drumlish, Ennybegs, Leggah, Rosduff and the countless other unremarkable, unattractive and scattered groups of dwellings which were the heartland of his support. The populace were largely backward, conservative folk, content to eke out a meagre existence much as their fathers and grandfathers had done. Yet there was a tradition of political intimacy of which Childers slowly became an accepted part. He took great pains to come to terms with the local scene, appearing at fairs to familiarise himself with cattle prices, inspecting drainage and associated machinery and seeking always to attract industry to the area.

Concern for home defence and safety was, quite naturally, of prime importance to everyone in Ireland after a State of Emergency was declared, but to Erskine Childers it was only the most immediate public manifestation of his interest in World War II. Wide international links, active participation of relatives and the broad international development of both Erskine's and Ruth's thinking ensured that the conduct and progress of the War was deeply absorbing and the whole Childers family shared a feeling of involvement. B.B.C. news bulletins were listened to as avidly as anywhere in Britain, and the expanding conflict was a regular dinner-table and drawing-room topic of conversation.

Because of the family's international character the suburban house in Rathgar was recurringly a place to which emissaries of the Allies came for Government-sanctioned, or -requested, hospitality when in Dublin. In this way, though he was only a back-bench Dáil Deputy, Erskine probably became one of the most well-informed of Irish politicians on the unfolding global drama of World War II. Representatives of General de Gaulle's Free French headquarters arrived to assess for themselves Ireland's neutral diplomacy, and Erskine B. Childers still recalls his father's face aglow at the chance to converse in a language he loved. Admiral Sir Andrew Cunningham was another remembered visitor, who told Erskine B. that his grandfather had saved England and Europe in the first World War because of *The Riddle of the Sands*. Randolph Churchill called once unexpectedly with a rather awkward message of greeting from his famous father about the respect that he had always held for Erskine senior.

Other visitors included American Air Force personnel visiting Dublin while on leave from bases in Northern Ireland and relatives taking a respite from front-line duties.

For instance, a Canadian cousin not yet thirty years of age appeared with hair already snow-white from his ordeal as an advance artillery spotter in the Battle of Monte Cassino. Erskine's abiding interest in the arts brought visitors from outside the world of war such as Leslie Howard the actor, who talked about everything under the sun to his host only days before he was shot out of the sky on a flight to North Africa. Prior to filming *Henry V*, Laurence Olivier called to seek advice on possible sources of supply in Ireland of period equipment such as saddles, armour, lances and crossbows needed before the Battle of Agincourt could be re-fought in the Wicklow countryside.

Perhaps the most portentous visit was that of Julian Huxley, who was in Dublin to converse with scholars at the Dublin Institute for Advanced Studies. With his aptitude for the crucial historical question, Erskine asked him if, when he was waiting with other scientists for the first atomic-bomb test in the New Mexico desert, they knew with certainty that it would not start a chain-reaction explosion around Earth and break pieces off this planet. Huxley became very still and after what seemed like an eternity answered quite simply, 'no'. The incident was witnessed by Erskine B. who believes that was the moment when the post-war age arrived in the Childers household. [5]

As de Valera concentrated on walking the tightrope of neutrality and most members of his Government were absorbed in dealing with the emergency, Erskine demonstrated time and again his capacity to look forward. Assuming the mantle of self-appointed back-bench prophet, he envisaged the changed conditions which would follow an end of hostilities. In a wide-ranging speech during the Budget debate in 1941 he outlined his hopes and fears. [6] Criticising both major political parties for allowing the country to attempt to live off the fat of the land rather than sacrifice the enjoyment of many things for the sake of reconstruction, he appealed for the formulation of a plan with which to face post-war conditions. Re-organisation of the Civil Service and establishment of an export organisation were among other measures advocated.

Expanding the theme of post-war planning Childers prepared a paper in 1942 calling for a new approach to education, improved ways of production and better use of leisure time, emphasising the part that voluntary organisations could play. He foresaw that peace would bring a new era of internationalism in many spheres of life through travel and aviation with international cartels and dictation by larger states. Increasing non-U.K. exports would be vital if Ireland was to survive as a free nation, and pedigree cattle and seed potatoes were suggested as the most promising fields for examination. Self-sufficiency was totally rejected. [7]

A conviction that had grown steadily since Erskine's university days was that the era of ultra-nationalism was past and the only hope for lasting peace was a breaking down of national barriers, real and artificial. At Lenamore, Co. Longford in April 1943 he forecast that after the War the prosperity of the Irish worker and the Englishman, the Dane and the German, would be more closely linked than ever before. [8] At Bray in December 1944 he warned that for the first time Ireland would have to fight for trade and that meant fighting for a reasonable standard of living in a world where economic activity had been distorted by the ghastly conflict then reaching its final stages. [9] On V.E. Day, 8 May 1945, at Rathmines Town Hall Erskine told the Irish Red Cross that that country's destiny was inextricably linked with the destiny of Europe, and the preservation of European civilisation affected the life and fortune of the humblest Irish citizen. [10] A few months later at St John's, Co. Roscommon he predicted that the following twenty years would probably be the most significant in the history of the world and second only to the first few years of the Christian era. [11]

Conscientious constituency work was rewarded at general elections in June 1943 and May 1944, when Childers held his seat, though each time with the lowest number of first-preference votes among the successful candidates. Appointment as Parliamentary Secretary to the Minister for Local Government and Public Health in March 1944 necessitated resignation from the Federation of Irish Manufacturers, and it was with genuine regret that he bade farewell to close involvement with the industrial life of the country.

Wartime, in a big-spending department with little money available and a dire shortage of materials, was not the most promising base from which to launch a ministerial career. Much work was out of the public eye and contributions to Dáil debates were necessarily restricted to departmental matters, often answering batteries of questions about housing, bridges, roads, canals, unemployment assistance and national health insurance.

Childers, however, was always careful to circulate copies of his constituency and other speeches to the newspapers and was upset if nothing was reported. Once he wrote to the Assistant Editor of the *Irish Times,* complaining that he was being ignored.

The Minister for Local Government, Seán MacEntee, was a Belfastman and a loyal friend and supporter of de Valera since the War of Independence who made his political reputation as Minister for Finance from 1932. The senior Parliamentary Secretary, Dr. Francis Ward, was a Monaghan deputy and he concentrated on health matters. Dealing with civil servants and local government officers Childers soon earned a name for administrative efficiency and an eye for detail. A review of the Local Authority audit system was initiated, refresher courses instituted for County engineers and the County engineering service was reorganised. Provision was made for non-skid standards for road materials and for the first time regulations laid down for the width, elevation and curvature of roads.

A measure for which Erskine Childers was largely responsible was the Public Libraries Act of 1947. Legislation was necessary to enable the State to accept the gift of the Irish Central Library for Students from the

Carnegie Trust but he seized the opportunity to insert additional provisions for library development which have had far-reaching consequences. The Act established a Library Council to take over and administer the Library and gave the Council powers to consult with, advise and assist local authorities on public library services, including, with the consent of the Minister, provision of financial aid from the central exchequer.

Dermot Foley, erstwhile Director of the Library Council, has no hesitation in stating that the Public Libraries Act 1947 provided the impetus for development of the library service from 1960 onwards, and he regards Childers as the man who gave respectability to libraries and the library service. Curiously, a quarter of a century later, the author of the measure overlooked it himself when he compiled his *curriculum vitae* at the time of the Presidential Election.

Though the post-war period is remembered as a time when affluent Englishmen paid flying visits to Dublin to enjoy a good steak, the years were no more easy for Ireland than other Western European countries, and shortages lingered on. Some bitter strikes took place. A bad harvest in 1946 led to bread rationing and the hard winter of 1946–7 was exacerbated by acute fuel shortages. The Fianna Fáil Government raised food subsidies against a background of rising prices and this led to increased taxes being introduced in an unpopular supplementary budget in October 1947. Allegations of ministerial involvement in the affairs of Locke's Distillery at Kilbeggan went the rounds. Above all a new and relatively sudden political challenge was coming from Clann na Poblachta, a hard-line Republican party formed after the death in prison of a hunger striker, Seán MacCaughey. The party leader was Seán MacBride, son of the 1916 patriot Major John Mac-Bride and the legendary Maud Gonne, an erstwhile Chief of Staff of the I.R.A. and later a winner of both Nobel and Lenin Peace Prizes.

After Clann na Poblachta had won two by-elections in 1947 and with dissension in the Labour Party, de Valera called a general election in February 1948. Though Fianna Fáil won sixty-eight seats and 41.9 per cent of the vote the gamble failed when National Labour coalesced with other opposition parties and formed an Inter-Party Government with John A. Costello of Fine Gael as Taoiseach (Prime Minister). Ireland thus had a change of administration for the first time in sixteen years and though Erskine Childers was successful in the reconstituted Longford–Westmeath constituency, with the fourth highest number of first-preference votes among fifteen candidates, he was now for the first time an opposition deputy. Ruth told a friend how he was taken to Leinster House by chauffeur-driven car only to return by the number 15 bus. Of more concern was the need to obtain a suitable job, and after a worrying period he became Dublin Manager of Blackwood Hodge, the large British-based engineering company.

Within a year of taking office the Inter-Party Government found itself embroiled in controversy over relations with Britain. The 1936 External Relations Act associated Ireland with the nations of the British Empire and was intended by de Valera to act as a bridge to help solve partition. It was criticised in some quarters as leaving doubt about Ireland's constitutional position and both Labour and Clann na Poblachta parties favoured its repeal. Nevertheless few outside the Cabinet were prepared for a Sunday newspaper report to the effect that repeal was imminent in September 1948. The Taoiseach who was visiting Canada confirmed during an after-dinner speech that the report was correct, thus leaving Fianna Fáil and many Fine Gael supporters dismayed, not least by the apparently inept way in which the whole matter had been handled.

Fianna Fáil did not oppose repeal but refused to partake in the celebrations on Easter Monday 1949 which marked the coming into force of the Republic of Ireland Act. Predictably Britain responded by passing the Ireland Act which effectively enshrined partition, as Mr de Valera had feared. Erskine Childers made it quite clear in a Dáil speech in July 1949 that he saw no benefit whatsoever emanating from the repeal and had been quite happy to let the situation continue for a number of years before further clarifying the constitutional position. He said he hoped that the Minister for External Affairs, Seán MacBride, would start thinking of a definite attitude and approach to the British Government and the North, consider future policy and what the Northern Ireland Government might expect future relationships to be. [12]

Throughout the 1940s the Childers family lived comfortably in Rathgar. Erskine was often away and domestic weekends were infrequent. When the weather permitted time was devoted to gardening, which he found relaxing and tackled strenuously. Despite food shortages it was possible to entertain regularly and throw an occasional party. Lord Glenavy (Patrick Campbell the journalist and T.V. personality) recalled one being given for the Marquis of Donegal to which one representative was invited from every conceivable Dublin activity. Jack Doyle represented boxing with Chief Petty Officer Campbell filling in for the Irish Marine Service. Any politicians entertained were those found to be most congenial rather than useful in political terms, though Erskine never got particularly close to any parliamentary colleagues. His devotion to Eamon de Valera, the man rather than some of his political tenets, was complete, though he was always deferential and called him 'Chief' rather than use his christian name.

A much valued and relaxing social 'date' for a number of years was the Sunday-evening gathering at Rockbrook, the Rathfarnham home of Lord and Lady Glenavy. Gordon Campbell (the second Baron and father of Patrick) came from staunch Unionist stock and had been educated at Charterhouse and Sandhurst, serving for some years in the Royal Engineers. A member of the Irish and English Bars, he became Secretary of the Department of Industry and Commerce from 1922 to 1932 and was subsequently a director of several leading Irish companies. Though twenty years older than Erskine he liked him and respected his political intelligence, despite his own Fine Gael sympathies.

The basic circle at the Glenavy evenings was small and included Norah McGuinness the artist, Shelah Richards the actress and producer (erstwhile wife of playwright Denis Johnston), Willy Ganly (a Bank of Ireland director) and his wife Eileen and Paul and Eithne MacWeeney. Paul MacWeeney, later Sports Editor of the *Irish Times*, recalled the scintillating quality of the conversation and the anticipation of meeting the most interesting person or people who happened to be in Dublin at any particular moment.

From the theatrical world Micheál MacLiammóir and Hilton Edwards attended periodically, as did Evie Hone the stained-glass artist, whilst here Erskine met for the first time the remarkable Sir Robert and Lady (Dorothy) Mayer and Bridges Adams, Director of the Shakespeare Theatre at Stratford-on-Avon, with each of whom a life long friendship was established. On the other hand he fell out violently one evening with the novelist Francis Stuart who was boasting of his activities in Berlin during the war. Sometimes Glenavy's acid tongue provoked a response from Childers, whom he teased unmercifully about Fianna Fáil and his 'Spanish-American gangster friend', but after a few tense moments the evenings invariably ended on a friendly note.

There is no record of Ruth's appearing at the Glenavy gatherings nor indeed is she mentioned in connection with constituency activities, even when transport was no problem. In the summer of 1946 she seized a chance to visit her family in New England for the first time in ten years, taking the eight-year-old twins, whose initial reactions to the hustle of American life formed the basis of an amusing article in the *Boston Globe*. Correspondence makes it clear that by this time she was not concerned about 'working for Ireland' nor her husband's 'hot-headed emotion' on the subject. 'I long ago discarded any feeling of national boundaries', she wrote to her elder son, also complaining that 'no one is interested in my worries'. 'Every letter I've had from Daddy is financial, assuming that I'm having a millionaire's holiday — I have never had a more miserable three months in my life.'[13] There had been disagreement concerning the desire of Erskine B. to leave Trinity College, Dublin and gain experience of manual labour in America before resuming his education — a move which his mother thoroughly approved. But Erskine was concerned that his son might never resume study and even more so that the tradition of working for Ireland might be broken.

All the Childers children were set exacting standards just as their father had been by his parents. Advent of war ruled out any thoughts of schooling in England and the three eldest attended a Quaker boarding-school at Newtown in County Waterford to which the twins were sent in 1948. On a visit to London 'Sheila', the fortune-teller, prophesied international lives for all the youngsters, a prediction that proved to be all too accurate.

After over twenty years the marriage of Erskine and Ruth had survived many strains and if it was not exactly on the rocks it certainly lacked the permanent and evolving spiritual closeness that characterised the union of the elder Erskine and Molly. With a husband dedicated to politics and five children split up and away from home before they were eighteen, Ruth complained that Christmas time was lonely. She devoted much time to writing, penning a series of witty articles about life in Ireland for the *Boston Globe*. A novel, *Boo! Garibaldi!*, failed to find a publisher but a children's book, *When Marylee was a Little Girl*, based on her own New England childhood, was published in 1948.

An article entitled 'How a New Englander runs an Old World Home in Dublin' in the *Boston Globe* on 12 February 1950 proved to be Ruth's last. Poignantly she reported a grand Christmas reunion for which all her five children had returned to Ireland. Obviously there was no mention of the fact that she was mortally ill, yet exactly a month later she died of cancer in Portobello Hospital, Dublin at the early age of fifty and on the day after her elder son's twenty-first birthday.

It is difficult to fully assess the influence that Ruth brought to bear on the life and career of Erskine Childers. Meeting him in adolescence a few weeks after his father's execution she dominated his development and helped shape his views and attitudes as only an older woman could. The romance flourished during the years in Cambridge and Paris when a return to Ireland might have been deferred. Though reverence for his father and deference to his mother's wishes never wavered, it was Ruth who projected the theory into practice. Gently she prodded Erskine back and supported all his efforts for recognition and entry into politics. Seeing Childers in 1947 for the first time in nearly twenty years Mervyn Roberts, his study companion at Gresham's School and contemporary at Cambridge, was struck by the change. The flamboyant and arrogant undergraduate that he remembered was now a concentrated man of action and quietly the master of his job. Mr Roberts believes that Ruth's responsibility was very great indeed.

A widower at the age of forty-four, Erskine was, perhaps, entitled to feel that life had dealt harshly with him. Yet as he toured Longford and Westmeath in the late spring of 1951, drumming up votes for the fifth time in thirteen years, he believed that his political fortunes might be on the mend. For the Inter-Party Government had fallen on the question of the Mother and Child Health Scheme proposals and Fianna Fáil scented victory in the ensuing general election. If the hopes matured into reality it seemed likely that he would become a full member of the Government for the first time.

Chapter VIII
GOVERNMENT
UNDER 'THE CHIEF'

The first Inter-Party Government is remembered essentially by its hasty repeal of the External Relations Act, echoes of which reverberated through Westminster and Stormont, and the Mother and Child controversy which has a secure place in the lore of Irish Church–State relationships. The second Inter-Party Government, without the radical influence of Clann na Poblachta, left little for posterity. Between the two a largely unremarkable Fianna Fáil administration, which lasted almost exactly three years and encountered serious balance-of-payments difficulties, gave Erskine Childers his first experience as a full government minister.

At the age of 45 as Minister for Posts and Telegraphs he was the youngest member of the Cabinet announced on 13 June 1951. Roughly half of his colleagues had served in successive Governments under de Valera since 1932, men who were closely associated with the elder Childers during the years 1919 to 1922. Ministries were shuffled, though Lemass, as Tánaiste (Deputy Prime Minister), remained at Industry and Commerce and Gerald Boland retained Justice. The only other new minister was Thomas Walsh at Agriculture. Approaching his seventieth year 'The Chief' retained much of his old mental and physical vigour, though his eyesight was causing great concern and he was to spend much of 1952 in hospital in Holland. His only political concession, however, was to appoint Frank Aiken to External Affairs, a portfolio he had previously retained himself.

An indication of the bitterness surrounding the fall of the first Inter-Party Government can be gauged by an episode soon after commencement of the Fourteenth Dáil during a debate on the Justice Department estimates. Patrick McGilligan of Fine Gael, who had just relinquished office as Minister for Finance, alluded to mutilation of a public document, alleging that 'a good deal of hanky panky has gone on with regard to a man who in this House is now masquerading as the Minister for Posts and Telegraphs'. Pressed further, McGilligan pointed at Childers and said, 'that man is masquerading as such if he was not a citizen of this country when he was elected to this House; and I do not believe he was a citizen when he was so elected'.[1]

The allegation sprang directly from an incident some months before when a deputation from Longford visited the Dáil to discuss provision of a technical school for the County. General MacEoin, then Minister for Justice, referred publicly to Childers as an English citizen. Afterwards MacEoin was told the facts and warned that any controversy about nationality would arouse bitter feelings among his constituents, but subsequent examination of the records revealed an apparent irregularity in the Official Register of Persons receiving Certificates of Naturalisation. Clearly Erskine's success in five consecutive elections when other local Fianna Fáil deputies had failed was a source of intense irritation and, desperate for mud to fling, MacEoin briefed McGilligan, who awaited his opportunity.

Gerald Boland explained to the Dáil that a clerical error had resulted in two pages of the Register being accidentally turned over together, adding bitterly that having murdered the father McGilligan now wanted to murder his son.[2] Echoes of the Civil War distressed Childers considerably as he sat silently on the Government bench but at a rally in Kilbeggan shortly afterwards he felt obliged for the first time to allude publicly to the circumstances surrounding his father's execution and his own citizenship.

After my father's trial I was permitted to see my father for about five minutes. He asked me whether I wished to take part in politics and when I replied in the affirmative he made me swear that I would shake the hand of all those who signed his execution warrant and that I would never allow the mention of his execution to be used in my presence as an incitement to Civil War bitterness. Everyone knows that I have carried out his wish as far as in me lies.

I am, however, compelled by the circumstances attending this despicable attack on my honour to refer to my father's death and the fact that he alluded to his nationality in his defence because of the slanders then being repeated that he was masquerading as an Irish patriot, while in reality being an English spy. When Mr McGilligan is given the facts I trust he will follow my father's example and try to assuage the bitterness caused by his unfortunate attack on the Government and on myself by some appropriate action. [3]

But more mud was flung on the final day of the Dáil session when Childers was accused by another opposition deputy of being a director of a company securing a contract from the Board of Works, whereas, of course, he resigned from Blackwood Hodge immediately on taking office. Yet if the general political scene brought irritation and frustration the new Minister determined to make his mark at the Department of Posts and Telegraphs, seizing the long-awaited chance to influence Irish lives in a direct way.

The small West Wicklow town of Baltinglass had few claims to fame prior to December 1950, when it achieved notoriety far beyond the shores of Ireland by demonstrating that the will of the people can triumph over bureaucracy. James Everett, then Minister for Posts and Telegraphs and a long-serving Wicklow deputy, approved a proposal to replace the retired Baltinglass sub-postmistress by a neighbour rather than her niece who had assisted her for many years. Local resentment was strong and a petition of protest was quickly organised by certain townsfolk, who included one of Field-Marshal Montgomery's former staff officers, a veteran of weightier battles such as El Alamein. Telephone poles were cut down, leaflets scattered from an aircraft over Dublin and extra police drafted to guard equipment. After the newly appointed sub-postmaster resigned the popular and obvious choice was eventually ratified by the Minister, leaving the image of the Department somewhat tarnished. The incident was another nail in the coffin of the first Inter-Party Government. No wonder 'Quidnunc' was moved to comment in the *Irish Times* that 'a new broom is badly needed at P & T':

The new Minister is far too clever to sweep too clean. I hope he will take a real interest in Radio Éireann which has been starved of funds. Mr Patrick Little, his Fianna Fáil predecessor ... was too gentle a person to fight his Department's corner against 'Finance'. The less I say about Mr Everett in relation to broadcasting the better. So let us hope that under Mr Childers Radio Éireann will flourish like the green bay tree.[4]

At the Departmental offices in the G.P.O. Building in Henry Street, where Radio Éireann studios were also located, Childers soon became acquainted in detail with the many difficulties facing him. Post Office activities were still largely governed by legislation dating from 1908 whilst Radio Éireann, founded in 1926, had suffered from being a virtual branch of the Civil Service and from the tight grip of the Department of Finance. Secretary of the Department of Posts and Telegraphs since 1946 was Leon O'Broin, a devout Roman Catholic of conservative outlook also a noted historian and author. From the beginning Minister and Secretary were frequently at variance after the former made it clear on day one that he had no intention of merely acting as a rubber stamp, was fully capable of judging departmental issues for himself and expected compliance and efficiency from his staff at all times. O'Broin did not appreciate Erskine's broad culture and overtly saw him as an Englishman who simply could not be expected to understand the Irish people.

Civil Service complacency was sorely tried as Childers set his restless imagination to work, and O'Broin found himself deluged with memoranda. A two-day sample gives an indication of the wide variety of ideas he put forward.

25 July 1951
A request to consider the feasibility of a single Telephone Directory for Northern Ireland and the Republic.
A suggestion that Ria Mooney, Shelah Richards and Hilton Edwards should be invited to make helpful suggestions for the improvement of Radio Éireann drama.
A suggestion that there should be a Radio Week to celebrate 25 years of Radio Éireann.
A request for preparation of a letter to Seán Moylan suggesting a conference with the Department of Education setting out subjects for discussion and a résumé of past experience.
A suggestion that the Thomas Moore Centenary should be marked with John McCormack recordings and a prize for rendering of Moore melodies.

26 July 1951
Details requested of news devoted to the Government and the opposition.
Information on the earnings of sub-postmasters.
A request to investigate claims that not enough attention was given by Radio Éireann to the Mansion House Anti-Partition Committee nor to Northern Ireland.
A request to examine a complaint regarding call-back to a 'phone subscriber.
A suggestion for a Radio Éireann series of famous people for districts of Ireland — for example in Longford:— Mrs Kate Meyrick, Gen. MacEoin, Mrs Cornwallis-West, Padraig Colum, Sir Henry Wilson, Maria Edgeworth and Oliver Goldsmith.

In acknowledging that Childers was by far the busiest of the five Longford–Westmeath deputies the *Longford News* contrasted his regular after-Mass Sunday speeches in the constituency with a reception held for the wedding of his eldest daughter Ruth in January 1952, which was attended by the 'elite and intellectual'. [5] But this was not an overly happy time for the family. The children were widely scattered, Erskine B. now married and living in Australia, Ruth settled in Yorkshire after her marriage, and Rory reading medicine at Trinity College, Dublin and spending much of his time in a flat near the city centre. Only the twins, playing up in rebellious fashion at their school in Hertfordshire, were still dependent and missing their mother very much indeed. Yet Erskine carried his years lightly and it was almost impossible to believe he had a grown-up family. Perhaps the boyish features were starting to convey something of a rueful look if he was caught off guard, the eyes quizzical, the smile a trifle hesitant as sadness left its mark. Yet unmistakably he was a highly eligible 'catch', if only he allowed himself a respite from work for long enough to be noticed.

Not that the fair sex had been absent from Erskine's life, for he enjoyed nothing more than the company of an intelligent woman. His good looks, innate courtesy and quiet, understanding manner appealed to the ladies and though small talk was scorned, an interest in food, drink and clothes made for ready conversation. Women found it easy to pour out their troubles to him. Erskine's unusual childhood and early marriage had precluded much normal adolescent fun. The responsibility of fatherhood combined with impecuniosity to limit social life both at Cambridge and in Paris so there had been no real opportunity to 'sow wild oats'. Hence, as he approached middle age, parties provided a welcome diversion and for a brief spell he enjoyed playing hard as well as working hard. But nothing like a permanent attachment was formed and at times he ached for the companionship and stability of married life.

At the beginning of 1952 Erskine chanced to meet the Assistant Press Attachée at the British Embassy in Dublin. Miss Margaret Dudley was the daughter of a Cork-born solicitor father and a Mayo mother and had grown up in the Ballsbridge district of Dublin. In her own words she had attended most schools in the city at one time or another before starting work in the office of Ireland's first Trade Union for Women and subsequently spending five years in the Welfare Department of the St John Ambulance Brigade. Her duties were largely connected with running three dining-rooms in the city of Dublin to feed expectant mothers suffering from malnutrition, for three months before birth and two months post-natally. Though such women were issued with food vouchers by the Government, many used them to feed other members of their family and James Larkin was mainly responsible for the concept of the dining-rooms, the first being located in a garage at the rear of Merrion Square. Larkin personally asked the St John Ambulance Brigade to undertake the work.

World War II gave Miss Dudley an opportunity to add a dimension to her life when she joined the British Civil Service in 1941, serving initially in Dublin at the office of Sir John Maffey (Lord Rugby) and later at the Irish Desk in the Empire Division of the Ministry of Information in London under Nicholas Mansergh. Any vestige of a parochial Dublin outlook, if it had ever existed, was dispelled in a war-weary British capital under siege from Hitler's rockets, added to which her flat was situated in the 'red light' district between Russell Square and St Pancras! After hostilities ceased and the Ministry of Information disbanded she served for a spell in the Persian Section of the Foreign Office before returning home to Dublin.

Erskine's discerning eye was quickly attracted by her fine intelligence, striking good looks and keen dress sense, a physical resemblance to the Duchess of Windsor having gained her the nickname 'Wallis' in London, while her broad culture and outlook struck an immediate chord. He even managed to get over the initial shock of finding a press attachée who could cheerfully admit to never having read any of his speeches! It came as no surprise to mutual friends to learn of their engagement but marriage presented something of a difficulty in the Dublin of 1952, for Miss Dudley, known to everyone as Rita, was a Roman

Catholic. During the long reign of Archbishop John Charles McQuaid mixed marriages were most definitely discouraged, no Nuptial Mass was permitted in the rare event of his permission being granted and the ceremony was required to take place in the sacristy or a private chapel, often very early in the morning. Such stringent and unnecessary conditions caused much resentment and the Dudley family had witnessed this furtive spectacle some time before when one of Rita's sisters had married a Protestant. All concerned determined to have no more of it and, more importantly, the bride herself quite naturally wished to be married in front of a high altar.

Representations to Archbishop McQuaid proved of no avail, to Rita's chagrin and Erskine's intense irritation. The prelate appeared to be most interested in finding an excuse for the fact that one of his flock should actually want to marry a non-Catholic, suggesting that she was 'without dowry' and it was her last chance of marriage. Erskine pondered on his own position and during a trip to Rome visited Cardinal Montini (later Pope Paul VI) for talks. Despite an all-night discussion which ended with Mass in the Sistine Chapel the Cardinal was unable to dispel many of the reservations Erskine had harboured for some thirty years, so there could be no question of a conversion. For her part Rita never ceased to be amazed by Erskine's knowledge of the history and theology of the Roman Catholic Church.

Ultimately it was reluctantly decided that there was no alternative but to marry outside Ireland and on 16 September 1952, after a civil ceremony, full Nuptial Mass was celebrated at the fashionable St Joseph's Church on Avenue Hoche in Paris. But the happy day had a decidedly Irish atmosphere. The bride was given away by her brother. The Irish Ambassador, Cornelius Cremin, acted as best man and his wife was matron of honour. The officiating priest was a Passionist who had trained at Mount Argus in Dublin, and guests included the Earl of Granard, the author Brian Inglis and some Irish tourists on their way back from Lourdes, one of whom sported a kilt. Greetings were received from the Cardinal Archbishop of Paris. After a reception at the Irish Embassy the couple departed in a Rolls Royce Silver Ghost, which was loaned by a friend but erroneously reported to be a gift from the bride, for a honeymoon at a château in the Médoc region owned by the Barton family. Some years later at a Pro-Cathedral reception in Dublin, Dr McQuaid appeared to go out of his way to bring Erskine and Rita a cup of tea, which they interpreted as a gesture of reconciliation.

With a ready-made family of five children, and grand-children soon to appear, Rita immediately assumed rather more responsibilities than most newly-weds but an in-defatigable spirit and impish sense of humour, which had enabled her to convince stiff-upper-lip British diplomats that her home was a little grey cottage in the west, carried her through the toughest of tests. It was thought impru-dent to continue in her job, the English connection having caused quite enough problems for Erskine, though Molly Childers in particular believed it was wrong for her daughter-in-law to forgo the chance of a good pension. At all events there was more than enough to do as a minister's wife, supporting her husband in all his endeavours and caring for his material comforts. Erskine was soon aware of not-so-subtle attempts to change some of his habits too and was gradually weaned away from cigarettes, of which he had been smoking far too many, in favour of a pipe.

Meanwhile, at the Department of Posts and Telegraphs it was the possibilities and potential of broadcasting that had initially most exercised the mind of the Minister. Broad-casting time was limited to only seven and a half hours a day, the licence fee was the lowest in Europe and the transmitters at Cork, Dublin and Athlone all needed replacing. Radio Éireann seemed hamstrung and some reorganisation was patently necessary. After an exhaustive investigation[6] Childers approached the Department of Finance with a brief on broadcasting policy and subse-quently obtained Cabinet approval for fundamental

His Excellency Erskine Hamilton Childers, fourth President of Ireland, 1974. Phot: Lensmen.

Three childhood photographs of Erskine Childers with his brother Robert.

The *Daily Sketch* front page for 25 November 1922, the day after the execution.

Above: Erskine with his father and brother on the beach at
Worthing, c.1919. Photo: Radio Times Hulton Picture Library.
Below: On holiday in France, c.1928.

Above: a family portrait c.1942. Erskine Childers with his younger son Rory at the rear, and in front with his first wife Ruth, his daughters Ruth, Margaret and Carainn, and his elder son Erskine Barton Childers.

Below: the formal photograph of the 1951 Fianna Fail Cabinet, in which Erskine Childers (back row, extreme right) was Minister for Posts and Telegraphs. The photograph includes two other future Presidents, Mr. Eamon de Valera, and (standing at the back, the highest in the group) Mr. Cearbhall Ó Dálaigh, then Attorney General.

A portrait taken after the marriage of Erskine Childers to Miss Rita Dudley by Fr. Leo Gribben of the Passionist Congregation at St. Joseph's Church, Avenue Hoche, Paris, on 16 September 1952.

Above: the formal picture of the 1959 Fianna Fail Cabinet, in which Erskine Childers continued in the position he held in the previous government, as Minister for Lands, for exactly a month, before becoming Minister for Transport and Power. Photo: Lensmen.

Below: Two cartoons from *Dublin Opinion* during his term as Minister for Lands.

" It's grown three-quarters of an inch
since I took over ! "

THE YOUNG MAN AND THE SEA

Erskine Childers as Minister for Transport and Power, and Posts and Telegraphs, with Brian Faulkner, the Northern Irish Minister of Commerce, signing the Electricity Power Link Agreement in Belfast in October 1967. Photo: *The Irish Times.*

Above: Erskine Childers when Tanáiste and Minister for Health at the Irish Embassy in London on the occasion of the launching of the Coole Edition of Lady Gregory's works on 4 May 1970. With him are (left to right) the Irish Ambassador Dr. Donal O'Sullivan, Sir Robert Mayer, and Colin Smythe.
Below: with Emma English of Limerick, the winner of a national anti-smoking poster competition in January 1971. Photo: *The Irish Press*.

Erskine Childers with Jack Lynch at the time of the Presidential nominations. Photo: Lensmen.

The inauguration ceremony of Erskine Childers as the fourth President of Ireland, in which the oath is administered by the President of the High Court, Mr. Andrias Ó Caoimh, with the Chief Justice, Mr. W. O'B. FitzGerald. Seated between Mrs. Childers and the President is the Taoiseach Mr. Liam Cosgrave.

Above: the first meeting between an Irish head of state and a member of the British Royal Family, at Summerhill College, Sligo, in August 1974; Bernard McDonagh, President Childers, Mrs. Childers, and Lord Mountbatten. Photo: Champion Art Studios, Sligo.

Below: receiving the Freedom of Sligo in August 1974, during the Yeats International Summer School, which the President had opened that year. With him are the Mayor of Sligo Councillor Patrick McLoughlin and Dr. John Kelly, Assistant Director of the School.

A family group at Áras an Uachtaráin on the occasion of the sixty-eighth birthday of the President, seen here with his second wife, Mrs. Rita Childers, and their daughter, Nessa, on 11 December 1973. Photo: *The Irish Press.*

The state visit of President and Mrs. Childers to Belgium. A photograph taken at a reception given in their honour by King Baudouin and Queen Fabiola.

President Childers with his last formal visitors to Áras an Uachtárain on Friday 15 November 1974, two days before his death. With him (from left to right) are M. Jean Sauvagnargues (the French Foreign Minister), M. Jacques Chirac (the French Prime Minister), Mr. Liam Cosgrave (the Taoiseach) and Dr. Garret FitzGerald (Minister for Foreign Affairs).

Mrs. Rita Childers laying a wreath on the occasion of the ecumenical service held to bless her husband's grave in Derralossary churchyard.

changes. On 5 November 1952 the Dáil learned that an Advisory Council of five people would be established to advise the Minister and take responsibility for the general control and supervision of the broadcasting service.[7] The Council would meet every fortnight with the Minister attending once a quarter, their relationship being similar to a Board of Directors and a controlling shareholder. Appointment of a new Director of Radio Éireann in the person of Maurice Gorham brought twenty-one years of B.B.C. experience to the job. After 1 January 1953 the status of Radio Éireann lay in between that of the ordinary Civil Service and an independent statutory organisation.

Erskine Childers maintained the closest interest in Radio Éireann and instigated an exhaustive analysis of programmes. As a lifelong lover of classical music he was the first Government Minister to publicly decry the lack of a Concert Hall in Dublin, though regular Sunday-night broadcast concerts were initiated from the Gaiety Theatre. The Radio Éireann Singers were formed and the Radio Éireann Symphony Orchestra was expanded under a full-time conductor. Inspired by Thomas Davis's saying, 'educate that you might be free', the first broadcast lecture was given in September 1953 by Professor Myles Dillon on the subject of the Irish language. With good reason the *Irish Times* commented that Erskine Childers seemed to be establishing himself as the cultural leader of the Government and that Radio Éireann had benefited immensely from his progressive leadership.[8]

Prospect of a national television service was already looming. By the end of 1951 it was estimated that about 500 sets were in use in east-coast districts of Ireland receiving British television, and the establishment of a B.B.C. transmitter in Belfast beamed Anglo-American 'sub-culture' to an even wider area of the Republic. In autumn 1953 Childers visited Brussels, Paris and London specifically to inspect television services and subsequently wrote to Leon O'Broin asking him to finalise the 'position with regard to television'. 'As a source of adult education,' he wrote, 'it is the last weapon we possess if we are to remain reasonably distinctive in character and temperament. The capital cost spread over eight years is not excessive.'[9] As Irish television commenced on 31 December 1961 it was clear that embryonic planning had taken place under Erskine Childers's direction.

Fianna Fáil lost four seats at the general election on 18 May 1954 and a second Inter-Party Government took office under John Costello on 2 June 1954. In Longford–Westmeath, where a young barrister called Brian Lenihan fought his first election for Fianna Fáil, Childers was elected without reaching the quota, though for once he did not have the lowest number of first preference votes among the successful candidates. Firmly at the helm of his Department he was thus out of office overnight, a fact which probably prompted his comment that it was the lowest point in national life since independence. At the height of his powers with visible results flowing from his innovative hand, Erskine's frustration was understandable and, unusually for the period, his successor Michael Keyes paid tribute in the Dáil to 'the wonderful amount of energy put into the Department by Deputy Childers with commendable success.'[10]

In his early days at Post and Telegraphs the Department had been approached by Pye, the Cambridge-based electrical and wireless manufacturing firm with a view to construction of a factory in Ireland. The request was of especial interest to the Minister as the Managing Director, C. O. Stanley, had at one time been connected with his brother Robert in a business venture. Stanley's story of success began as office-boy in the local bacon factory at Cappoquin in County Waterford, and he had progressed to become head of one of the largest concerns of its type in Britain. It fell to Michael Keyes to formally open the new Pye Factory at Finglas in June 1956, but Erskine Childers was also present in his new capacity as Managing Director of Pye Telecommunications in Ireland. Based at the Dundrum headquarters he spearheaded the sale of two-way mobile radios for use in vehicles such as ambulances and police cars, at airports (ground to air), at sea and in radio links such as are used by the Post Office. Much of the country was covered in the Volkswagen 'beetle' which had replaced the chauffeur-driven government car and in which huge mileages were recorded.

Though he missed the challenge of government there were some compensations for Erskine, who was revelling in a warm and secure home life. He and Rita often tramped across the Dublin Mountains at week-ends combining exercise with an opportunity to discuss everything under the sun without interruption by the telephone or casual callers at the house. Part of each summer was spent at Glendalough House, where his mother now lived permanently, and some enjoyable holidays were spent abroad. Arrival of a daughter, Nessa, changed the pattern of life but set the seal on an ideal marriage. All of this had a mellowing effect on Erskine, whose interest in spiritual matters revived during this period. A tentative return to churchgoing gradually crystallized into a deep Christian commitment, Anglican ritual and dogma now presenting little problem.

As the Inter-Party Government grappled with industrial and agricultural stagnation, a balance-of-payments deficit and rising unemployment, which prompted a fresh wave of emigration to Britain, only the Minister for Finance, Gerard Sweetman, inspired any confidence. Realising that economic expansion was the only solution to the country's problems, he was instrumental in appointing a brilliant young economist to be Secretary of his Department, believing him to be the person most capable of planning for the future. That T. K. (Ken) Whitaker hailed originally from Rostrevor in County Down was purely coincidental, and few could have foreseen the longer-term consequences of the appointment in May 1956.

In addition to economic difficulties another problem was growing as a fresh wave of I.R.A. activity, 'Operation Harvest', commenced with a series of explosions in border areas in December 1956. The Northern Ireland Government promptly introduced internment without trial, which led to an upsurge of Republican sympathy in the South. Speaking at Granard Childers made no secret of his contempt for what was happening, recalling that I.R.A. bombs in London in 1939 destroyed good work and postponed unity for years.

Blowing up transformers and buses in the Six Counties was like bringing back horses to replace tractors or flying tricolours from every house to prove that the residents were Irish. During the war the same group had imperilled neutrality by conspiring with one of the warring countries whilst after the war the same group had achieved a 26-county Republic by agitation in the Dáil.[11]

At the March 1957 general election following the fall of the Inter-Party Government, a number of Sinn Féin candidates stood on an abstentionist policy and won four seats to give the party its first successes since 1927. In Longford–Westmeath Rory Brady, a young schoolmaster who had led the I.R.A. raid on Arborfield Barracks near Reading in August 1955, polled 365 more first-preference votes than Erskine Childers, both men being elected on the seventh count. At one point the count at Mullingar Courthouse got so rough that Rita Childers was advised to depart quickly through a rear window. Nationally Fianna Fáil was returned to office with a highest ever total of 78 seats and its first over-all majority since 1944, and, with a clear mandate to enforce the law, introduced internment in July 1957, when 60 men were arrested in the Republic. Thereafter the I.R.A. campaign gradually fizzled out until it was officially called off in February 1962, by which time both Northern and Southern Irish Goverments had abandoned internment.

A spell of just over two years as Minister for Lands, Forestry and Fisheries from 1957 to 1959 provided Childers with few opportunities to directly influence the everyday lives of the Irish populace. From the start he made it clear that henceforth waste land would not be tolerated and he determined that Ireland would no longer be content to remain the European country with the lowest number of privately owned forests. With a climate and soil more favourable to tree-growing than almost anywhere else in Europe the reafforestation of Ireland and fostering of industries such as paper-making and -packaging, and even the ultimate export of timber, all seemed viable. Increased grants were provided to encourage investment in tree-growing and industrial consultants were employed to apply work-study techniques to forestry operations in order to improve productivity and devise a better method of rewarding workers. The resultant Incentive Bonus Scheme which related to a catalogue of forestry work-values proved highly successful as production soon increased by 40% and wages rose by up to 20%.

Fishery aspects of the portfolio provided equal potential for development, though the Minister humbly admitted at a London Press Conference that his own experience of fishing had been confined to the streams of Wicklow. A re-organisation of Bord Iascaigh Mhara (the Sea Fisheries Board) enabled bulk shipments of haddock and hake to be despatched direct from Dunmore East, Co. Waterford to Billingsgate Market in London, while increased grants and loan facilities were arranged for owners of fishing-vessels. Technical advice and marketing-support were improved and training schemes started for skippers and crews. On a visit to Spain Childers tried unsuccessfully to persuade the Spanish Government and private industrialists of the merits of a fish-processing plant in Cork or Kerry which could be serviced by the fleets regularly fishing off Ireland's south-west coast. His only reward was to be invested with the Grand Cross of the Order of Civil Merit by General Franco at the Prado Palace in Madrid.

Mr de Valera's Cabinet after 1957 included new members such as Jack Lynch at Education, Kevin Boland at Defence and Neil Blaney at Posts and Telegraphs. The founder generation of Fianna Fáil was gradually bowing out and departure of 'the Chief' himself, now in his mid-seventies, could not be long delayed. This was effected by the need to find a successor to President Seán T. O'Kelly, whose second seven-year term expired in 1959. But Dev sought one further political change before he left the Dáil, and accordingly set about the introduction of a single-vote system, as in Britain. He had been tempted to incorporate this in the 1937 Constitution but refrained lest controversy on this aspect led to defeat of the package as a whole. Experience of the two Inter-Party Governments re-inforced a belief that the transferable-vote method of proportional representation, a legacy of British rule (PR was introduced at the very end of British rule in Ireland on the grounds that Irish needs and conditions were quite distinct from Britain's) that remained popular with the Irish people, caused weak and unstable coalitions that were bad for the country.

Erskine Childers was one deputy who was elected on the second- and third-preference votes of other candidates, as evidenced by the numerous occasions he had scratched home on the final count. But he spoke in favour of the single vote in the Dáil, saying that proportional representation was not natural to men and women who wanted their country to be governed wisely and firmly. He rounded on James Dillon for stating that Ireland was different to Britain as people on both sides of the House had shot at each other, and reminded him that everyone was trying to forget whatever bitterness was left from the Civil War.[12]

But the legacy of bitterness ran too strongly for some of the erstwhile participants to forget. Shortly before his death in 1975 Ernest Blythe told the author that Frank Aiken had not spoken to him for fifty years and always turned the other way if they met. Ironically de Valera's opponent in the 1959 Presidential election, General Seán MacEoin, was the man who had proposed him as President in 1921, though the two men had been on different sides virtually ever since. General MacEoin, who lost by 111,740 votes when he contested the Presidency against Seán T. O'Kelly in 1945, was another man who, apparently, could not forget.

When the people of Ireland went to the polls in May 1959 they were voting for a President and the future system of electing Dáil Deputies, since the Constitution can only be amended after a referendum. Mr de Valera was successful by a large majority but his concept of the single-vote system was rejected. As for Erskine Childers, he could only wonder if his ambition to become Minister for Agriculture might now be realised in the necessary Government re-shuffle.

Chapter IX
ONE OF THE LEMASS
INVINCIBLES

Ending of the long political reign of Eamon de Valera, extending back to 1917 as Member of Parliament, Dáil Deputy, President of the Executive and leader of Fianna Fáil, might be assumed to have left a void. Yet, though Dev was a legend in his own lifetime, nothing could have been further from the truth, politically speaking, in 1959. Indeed, a retrospective view gaining credence in the early 1980s suggests that progress in the country may have been delayed because de Valera remained on as Taoiseach for so long. Seán Lemass, Tanaiste since 1945 and universally acknowledged as successor, already enjoyed effective control of economic matters. Erskine Childers's own words can best summarise the complementary roles of the two leaders:

De Valera raised the spirit of the people and exhorted them to believe in their destiny as a separate people of ancient origin. Seán Lemass was the driving force in persuading people to use their talents and initiative to make Ireland a place where eventually everyone could find opportunities for living a full life. [1]

In 1958 Fianna Fáil agreed a programme of economic expansion covering the years to 1963, based on a paper prepared by Dr T. K. Whitaker, Secretary of the Department of Finance, and principally concerning the contribution of the State. This envisaged increased growth in national production, embracing industry, agriculture, tourism, electricity, transport, and exports and imports.

Having asserted just before the presidential election that 'the historic task of this generation is to secure the economic foundation of independence', Lemass's first task as Taoiseach was to reinforce the commitment to the programme. At Industry and Commerce his successor, Jack Lynch, rapidly concluded that the Department embraced far too many semi-State bodies and a division of responsibilities was overdue.

Thus, on 23 July 1959, exactly a month after assuming office, Lemass announced the formation of a new Department of Transport and Power with Erskine Childers as the Minister responsible. He had requested the Agriculture portfolio but the Taoiseach was adamant and later reputedly said he thought Childers would have been merely an armchair Minister for Agriculture.

The offices of the new Department remained in the Industry and Commerce building in Kildare Street, so that the division of personnel was easy, but Childers insisted to Mr Lynch that he only wanted staff who would be efficient. He established a precedent by appointing a lady to the position of Permanent Secretary for the first time. Miss Thekla Beere, daughter of a Church of Ireland clergyman and a graduate of Trinity College, Dublin, had entered the Civil Service in 1928 and risen by sheer ability to become an Assistant Secretary in the Department of Industry and Commerce in December 1953. She had known the Childers family for 25 years and as a founder member of An Óige had worked closely with Ruth for a period. A Doctorate of Laws Degree was conferred on her in 1960 by Dublin University in recognition of her distinguished career.

Semi-State companies supervised by the Department of Transport and Power included the Electricity Supply Board, Aer Lingus, Bord na Móna (Turf Development Board), Shannon Free Airport Development Company, Irish Shipping Limited and Coras Iompair Éireann (Irish Transport Company). The latter, largest and by far the most controversial, was already in the throes of a reorganisation under the terms of the 1958 Transport Act, which required it to become self-supporting by 31 March 1964. The Chairman, Dr C. S. Andrews, formerly Chief Executive of Bord na Móna, had a brief to restore Irish railways to a sound financial basis and was undertaking a stringent review of services that resulted in closure of un-economic lines and led to strident criticism. An unkind wag suggested that an appropriate greeting for Erskine's Christmas cards would be 'Hark the Herald Angels sing, Closing branch lines is the thing', but in reality his brother-in-law had suffered redundancy as a result of C.I.E.'s rationalisation and the Minister was far from indifferent to the human hardship caused.

Tourism was not initially a direct responsibility, though much work was associated with promoting travel. At a London Embassy reception in September 1959 the new Minister defined his four main priorities as making sure that Irish Shipping grew, ensuring maximum co-operation between C.I.E. and British Railways, improving motor-car ferry services to Ireland and securing full implementation of the 1958 Transport Act — adding that he was also much concerned about the projected growth of Shannon. Shortly after, at an Irish Tourist Association lunch in Dublin, breaking convention by speaking between the main and dessert course so as to be in the Dáil for the start of business, he confirmed that provision of a ferry service for vehicles across the Irish Sea was paramount. 'Men who will get things done, who will not be satisfied with talk only, but who will go into action,' he said, 'are good for the country.'[2]

One of many characteristics inherited from his father was a propensity to look ahead and endeavour to envisage life in the future, often with a remarkable degree of accuracy. At the beginning of the century the elder Erskine used *The Riddle of the Sands* to warn of the German threat, speaking and writing much to highlight the inadequacy of British army and naval forces in the event of conflict. His son envisaged a federation of European states as essential for

world peace and stability years before the Schuman Plan
and 1951 Treaty of Paris which set up the Coal and Steel
Community, forerunner of the E.E.C. He realised the enormous potential of television, telephones, computers and
other technology and tried to anticipate the effect which
they would have on individual lives.

A Fianna Fáil audience was treated to a peep into the
future in 1959, Childers forecasting that the 1970s would
bring arterial highways with 24 ft wide dual carriageways,
trains running at average speeds of 70 m.p.h. and modern,
silent buses co-ordinating with train services. Hovercraft,
he suggested, would ply the Irish Sea at speeds of 70 knots,
with people coming on day trips from Britain with cars.
All-in tickets would cover road and rail travel and hotels.
Freight traffic would be by way of containers with con-
veyors reducing handling and costs. Dublin Airport ter-
minal and apron facilities would double, and supersonic
flights to New York at 2500 m.p.h. would be possible with
vertically rising jet aircraft. [3]

Childers soon found himself facing a plethora of Dáil
questions concerning railway closures and other detailed
aspects of transport operation, to virtually all of which he
could only reply that these were matters in which he had
no function. Sometimes he would be drawn to give information but more usually was forced to adopt an uncomfor-
table position between baying opposition deputies and
sensitive semi-State companies. He endeavoured to clarify
the position once and for all by defining Ministerial and
Parliamentary control of public enterprise when presenting the Transport and Power Estimates in June 1960. [4]
Quoted in *A Source Book of Irish Government* the statement
has become something of a model.

As the only Protestant Fianna Fáil deputy and sole
Protestant member of successive Governments, Erskine
Childers rarely alluded to the fact and certainly made
nothing of it. Once, in March 1946, he spoke out publicly
after Edmund Warnock, Minister of Home Affairs at
Stormont, stated that Protestants were unhappy and did

not prosper in the South. Warnock was challenged to make a tour of the Twenty-Six Counties and then repeat the statement, Childers pointing out that they lived in an atmosphere of complete tolerance and their share in industrial and commercial activity far exceeded the proportion of their numbers. He also emphasised the absence of any form of religious test in connection with Government and local appointments. Many of the Childerses friends in private life were members of the minority Churches and Erskine must have unconsciously helped to make them feel part of the Nation and even to reconcile them to Fianna Fáil. The first Inter-Party Government left many Protestants dismayed by Fine Gael's clumsy handling of the repeal of the External Relations Act and the Mother and Child Health Scheme. There was a feeling, not strictly true, that Dev had subsequently stood up to the Roman Catholic Bishops and in a choice between Republican principle and Catholic principle, to use the words of the late Jack White, the erstwhile unionists would finish on the Republican side.[5]

Religious persuasion is of more relevance in County Monaghan than the rest of the Republic and strong residual links with the Orange Order and 'B' Special Constabulary existed in 1961. As one of nine counties of the ancient Province of Ulster, it might have found itself under a Belfast Parliament. When delegates to the Imperial Conference met in London iń July 1914 to decide the area allowed to secede from a Home Rule Dublin Parliament, it is said that Redmond offered all the nine counties to Carson, who refused because he thought it would speed the time when the excluded territory would vote itself back in. Monaghan has always possessed one of the largest Protestant populations in the South, though it is a shrinking number. As the total population of the County declined from 65,131 to 47,088 between 1926 and 1961, Protestants dwindled from 13,956 to 6,380 (21.5% to 13.7%). An influential Protestant Association returned candidates to the County Council and District Councils and for some

years had its own Dáil deputy in the person of Alex
Haslett, once Chairman of the Leinster House Kitchen
Committee. Ernest Blythe represented Sinn Féin/Cumann
na Gaedheal from 1918 to 1933 but up to 1961 no
Protestant had ever been returned on a Fianna Fáil
ticket.

At the March 1957 general election Monaghan, which
shares a border with three of the Six Counties, returned
James Dillon (Fine Gael), Patrick Mooney (Fianna Fáil) and
a Sinn Féin member who did not take his seat. Dillon, now
Fine Gael leader, had been entrenched since 1937 but
Fianna Fáil were anxious to regain a second seat and
Erskine Childers came into the reckoning as someone of
suitable standing and reputation, capable of garnering
Protestant support from the north of the County as well as
retaining the traditional Republican vote in the south. For
the first time it was all-important to Fianna Fáil that he was
a Protestant. Objections from Longford–Westmeath at the
loss of a long-standing member proved to be of no avail,
and Childers was adopted at a convention in Carrickma-
cross in June 1961, to the especial chagrin of Dr Francis
Ward, who had been a Fianna Fáil deputy from 1927 to
1948. In the event Ward contested the October 1961
election as an independent but was unsuccessful, as
Dillon, Mooney and Childers were elected. Rita Childers's
strongest recollection of this and the subsequent count in
1965 was of James Dillon's booming voice.

Over all the 1961 general election brought a loss of eight
seats to Fianna Fáil, who remained in power only with the
support of Independents. But though the Government
lived dangerously it was to lay the foundation of economic
independence and prosperity. A second and more comprehensive Programme for Economic Expansion drawn up
for the years 1964 to 1970 included detailed projections for
the private sector and provided for continuing consul-
tations with the main organisations representing different
interests. This turned the tide of emigration and brought
a rising population for the first time in over a century.

Lemass retained his Cabinet, promoting his son-in-law Charles Haughey to replace the deceased Oscar Traynor as Minister for Justice and appointing Kevin Boland as Minister for Social Welfare. Most welcome for Childers was the transfer of responsibility for tourism from Industry and Commerce to Transport and Power on 31 October 1961, filling a vacuum in Ministerial life whereby he seemed at times to be merely a mouthpiece for various semi-State boards. He delighted in a more comprehensive brief where his expertise as a former professional would be invaluable. Hoteliers, travel agents and officials soon became familiar with the words, 'when I was a travel agent in Paris', preceding reminiscences relating to a point in a speech or lecture.

Erskine related to tourism in an especially personal way. The Irish Tourist Board (An Bord Fáilte) was formed in 1938 and operated several representative offices overseas. Priority was given to ensuring that maximum funds were available and these increased steadily from £½M in 1960 to £5¼M in 1969/70. A study of the structure of tourism revealed too great a tendency to look to Dublin and in 1962 eight Regional Tourism Organisations were established in order to improve co-ordination at local level. These were independent limited companies funded by Bord Fáilte and led to the setting up of a network of tourist offices providing information and a free room-reservation service for visitors.

Conditions looked favourable for expansion in tourism. Ireland was peaceful and in the words of British Premier Harold Macmillan the population of the neighbouring island had never had it so good. Incomes were rising, overseas holidays were within reach of the working man's pocket, the number of private cars on the roads was increasing and air travel becoming commonplace. Talks were in progress between the Irish Department of Transport and its British counterpart, also with British Railways, which led to the introduction of car ferries on both Holyhead-to-Dún Laoghaire and Fishguard-to-

Rosslare routes in 1965. In that year too the British monopoly of passenger sea-transport across the Irish Sea was broken when Erskine Childers persuaded the Irish Government to purchase the B & I Steam Packet Company from Coast Lines Limited. An ambitious modernisation programme for B & I included car ferry vessels, Ro-Ro freight operations and a new management structure.

The farmhouse accommodation concept was energetically promoted and 1965 brought Government approval for grants for supplementary holiday accommodation in western areas. Development of State forestry for tourism purposes and provision of forest walks, nature trails and forest parks, such as that at Lough Key in County Roscommon, encouraged by Childers as Minister for Lands, was continued. He personally promoted the concept of Mediaeval Banquets which have proved so popular at Bunratty and Knappogue Castles in County Clare and Dunguaire Castle in County Galway. Frequently his deep reserves of knowledge surprised officials and audiences. When he opened a youth hostel in West Cork in July 1965 all present were amazed by his discourse on the history and geography of the remote Beara Peninsula in which he revealed intimate acquaintance with the region. Neither Minister nor Permanent Secretary forgot their associations with An Óige and Allihies was the first hostel built under a new grant scheme. Both took a keen interest when the International Youth Conference was held in Ireland in 1963. Dr Beere later became President of An Óige and Erskine was made a life member in 1973.

Dr Beere found her Minister easy to work with and recalls that he was good and considerate to staff. The voracious appetite for statistics did not diminish but he found certain technical aspects of energy difficult to grasp and of little interest. The eye for details extended to clothes and food, keenly observing what people wore and ate. Popularisation of fish as a socially acceptable dish rather than something associated with religious penance owes something to Erskine Childers. He took every opportunity to promote the possibilities for *haute cuisine* cookery so far as fresh- and sea-water fish available in Irish waters were concerned.

Foreign visits were an integral part of a Transport Minister's job. In December 1962 Ireland joined the Conference of European Transport Ministers which had been formed in 1953 and met twice yearly to discuss matters of common interest and co-ordinate activities. One meeting always took place in Paris and the other in the country of its President, who held office for one year. In this way Childers visited or re-visited many European cities for conferences and Dr Beere recalls him addressing gatherings in impeccable French on several occasions. During a Bordeaux conference he chose to forgo a visit to Toulouse where the Concorde supersonic aircraft was in the embryonic stages of development to call on his kinsman Ronald Barton, who lived not far away. Here too some enjoyable vineyard parties took place and Erskine was admitted as a Knight of the Vine. An amusing misunderstanding occurred at one conference when he alluded to his experiences as a travel agent, mentioning big-game hunting. Delegates blinked and sat up, and there was puzzlement apparent on some faces. The small, mild-mannered Irish Minister was suddenly regarded with renewed interest and listened to more intently. It was only when Dr Beere was subsequently asked how she enjoyed working for a big-game hunter that the confusion became apparent.[6]

Artistic festivals have become an ever more popular facet of tourism since World War II and the Yeats Summer School in Sligo annually attracts visitors from numerous countries. As someone who all his life found solace in reading poetry, Erskine Childers was an obvious choice to open the first School in August 1960. The organisers were so impressed that he was invited again a year later to read works by Yeats, Pearse, Stephens and W. H. Auden's works on Yeats, drawing on his own memories of Auden at Gresham's School. Describing himself as a dilettante who

130

had never made a serious study of Yeats, he recalled once hearing him chanting poetry, and also his own parents discussing with the great man whether poetry should be recited or chanted. At Erskine's suggestion Micheál MacLiammóir chanted some of Yeats's works in the Yeats Room at Sligo's Great Southern Hotel to an international audience. The *Irish Times* was moved to comment that 'Micheál MacLiammóir and Erskine Childers were a credit to our country ... the evident friendship that exists between them and appreciation of each other was a delight to watch'.[7]

An event close to Erskine's heart was the move to bring *Asgard* permanently to Ireland. When it was learned that she was for sale at Southampton a campaign was started by the *Sunday Review* newspaper, encouraged by the Marquis of Headfort. Colonel A. T. Lawlor, father of the Irish Naval Service, approached the Taoiseach, and Government approval was eventually given. Thus, on a July day in 1961, almost exactly 47 years since she sailed into Howth laden with arms and ammunition for the National Volunteers, President de Valera, Government Ministers and the Childers family headed a distinguished gathering at the little harbour to welcome back the diminutive craft in very different circumstances. The first tangible recognition of the elder Erskine's work for Ireland gave immense pleasure to his sons and the elderly and very frail Molly, to whom the President sent the Nation's loving greetings.

The Irish Government was not motivated solely by sentiment and the 56-year-old *Asgard* began a new life as a training vessel for the Naval Service, based at Crosshaven on Cork harbour. Five years later a move to preserve her on the hard at Howth was considered premature and strongly resisted. In February 1968 a Committee (Coiste an Asgard) was set up under the Chairmanship of Frank Lemass, brother of the Taoiseach and General Manager of C.I.E., and in March 1969 *Asgard* was commissioned as a training vessel for young people, which was the expressed wish of Molly Childers.

Molly, an invalid virtually all her life, died in January 1964 at the age of 87, when her husband's efforts and sacrifice were beginning to be widely recognised. Her elder son had faithfully carried out parental wishes to devote his life to Ireland and always used his influence in the name of moderation and reconciliation. Her younger son was enjoying a successful business career in England. Throughout their lives the brothers and their families moved freely across the Irish Sea, equally at home in both islands and having an intense love for each. How wide of the mark was Sir Horace Plunkett who wrote in his diary on 17 November 1922, 'if Erskine Childers is killed a widow remains to bring up two fine boys to hate England and sacrifice their lives too'.

The early 'sixties brought a period of contented family life that Erskine cherished and kept as private as possible. Rita was a wonderful companion, devoting herself to her husband and his career, sharing his idealism, encouraging all his endeavours, sometimes critical yet always constructive. Daughter Nessa brought continuing joy, demonstrating at an early age that she possessed a mind and character of her own. The children of Erskine's first marriage had all married by 1962 and resided in various parts of Europe or America. Elder son Erskine B. Childers probably spoke for them all when he remarked that no matter where he was his father had a firm grasp of the local scene and his paternal advice was always invaluable.

Erskine B. was himself ensuring that the name was not forgotten in Britain where he had become well known as a current-affairs commentator and interviewer on B.B.C. radio and television. A specialist in Middle East affairs, he was the author of two books on this contentious topic, finding expression in the written word like his grandfather. After his first appearance following the inception of Irish television, Erskine Childers asked the R.T.E. interviewer how he had got on. 'Fine,' came the reply, 'in fact if you worked on it, in a couple of years' time you'd be nearly as good as your son'! Younger son Rory was by this time settled in Chicago and his reputation as a cardiac specialist was to become world-wide. For some years Christmas brought a grand family re-union in Dublin and the walls of the Rathgar villa must have been near to bulging as newly arrived grandchildren swelled the numbers annually. With so many earlier Christmases overshadowed by sadness or insecurity Erskine anticipated and savoured these gatherings with almost childish delight.

The Department of Transport and Power made a full contribution to the economic resurgence and outreach which characterised the Lemass years and Fianna Fáil lived up to its slogan as the party of reality. Industry expanded rapidly as protection gave way to freer trade. The Control of Manufacturers Act was repealed and foreign industry encouraged to set up as the foundations were laid for some boom years. Tourism was one of many areas that grew as the Taoiseach looked beyond Ireland in political as well as economic terms. Membership of the European Economic Community was first unsuccessfully sought in 1961 and in a speech at the opening of Cork Airport in October that year Mr Lemass reiterated his commitment.

We are not seeking to join the E.E.C. as any sort of poor relation but as a developing country which studied all the implications and consequences of membership. The new airport at Cork symbolizes our purpose and will help us in our desire to have the world see us as a modern, progressive State coming rapidly and fully into line with all others in modern equipment and facilities. [8]

As a preparatory step towards the desired E.E.C. membership attempts were made to persuade the British Government to review the somewhat unfair trading relationship, particularly in regard to agriculture. These were unsuccessful until the advent of Labour under Harold Wilson in October 1964 when the climate changed and an Anglo-Irish Free Trade Agreement was signed in December 1965. Return to Ireland of the Casement remains from Pentonville Prison was an added bonus. Yet Childers, who knew and understood the British mind better than any of his colleagues, was not involved in these or any other inter-Governmental negotiations during the 1960s. Periodic nostalgic visits were made to Westminster for meetings of the Anglo-Irish Parliamentary Group, which he addressed in November 1967, whilst British Cabinet Ministers often shared St Patrick's Day festivities in London, Liverpool or elsewhere.

No Irish Minister was a more enthusiastic supporter of E.E.C. membership than Childers, and students at Queen's University, Belfast in December 1961 learned of his faith that it would pave the way for eventual re-unification. At the same venue earlier in the year all-Ireland transport had been the subject of his talk. This theme was broadened in October 1963 at Newry where, as the first Dublin Minister to address a Northern Irish Chamber of Commerce, he suggested a 'Come to Ireland' campaign under the joint auspices of Bord Fáilte and the N.I. Tourist Board.

On a private visit with Rita to Captain Peter Montgomery at Blessingbourne, near Fivemiletown in County Tyrone, Childers hoped to make history by becoming the first Southern Irish Minister to be received by Lord Brookeborough. Montgomery, a graduate of Trinity College, Cambridge and erstwhile conductor of sundry B.B.C. orchestras, rang Colebrooke to see if the Stormont Prime Minister would receive his guests. But the idea of entertaining even a Protestant Minister from the Republic struck terror into the heart of the venerable gentleman, who pleaded a previous engagement. An invitation was subsequently received from his son, Captain John Brooke, to take tea at near-by Ashbrooke, and the journey thence entailed passing in front of Colebrooke House. In the dusk of the winter afternoon Lord Brookeborough was observed sitting by the window reading with the aid of a table-lamp.

In summer 1965 Harry West, Stormont Minister of Agriculture, met Childers in the middle of the Woodford Canal on the boundary between Cavan and Fermanagh. The two conversed from their respective rowing-boats and agreed that Lough Erne should be linked to the Shannon water-way. Sadly the proposal was overtaken by events and came to nought. Elsewhere the uncrowded inland water-ways were alive with activity as boating enthusiasts sought refuge from the crowded Norfolk Broads.

But such cross-border forays were as nothing compared with the epoch-making visit by Seán Lemass to Stormont in January 1965 for lunch with Captain Terence O'Neill, the new Northern Premier. The seemingly impossible was made possible by Dr Ken Whitaker's friendship with O'Neill's Private Secretary, James Malley, and the generous spirit of the two Prime Ministers. A few weeks later Capt. O'Neill paid a reciprocal visit to Dublin and as a result various inter-departmental contacts were estab-lished. One of the first involved Erskine Childers, who received Brian Faulkner, Northern Minister of Commerce, in Dublin, and their talks resulted in formation of a com-mittee to plan a North–South electricity power link. An agreement was formally signed in Belfast in October 1967 by Childers and Faulkner and the link itself became operative in 1970, only to cease later as a result of I.R.A. activity. After the signing Erskine visited Ballylumford Power Station.

Another visit to Belfast took place in connection with tourism and in particular the joint promotion of hotels in the North and South. One minor item agreed was that paintings by Northern and Southern artists should be hung together in hotel lounges. On this occasion Erskine and Rita stayed on overnight, a gesture much appreciated by William Craig the Northern Home Affairs Minister, with whom they had supper. Other members of the Dublin party had raced back south to enjoy a convivial evening at a well-known restaurant near the Border.

The relationship between Seán Lemass and his Minister for Transport and Power was cordial but far from close. Erskine's loyalty was absolute but he was uneasy in his dealings in a way he had never been with Dev. If Lemass sought an opinion he expected brief, direct answers whereas Childers liked to cover all aspects of a matter and could become long-winded. Hence he was not consulted privately very much, though Lemass admired his competence and hard work despite finding him difficult to understand on occasions. Once, sitting next to Rita Childers at a dinner the Taoiseach questioned the value of the statistics collated and quoted so freely by her husband, doubting the benefit of third-level education — Lemass himself, of course, had left school at the age of sixteen to take part in the Easter Rising and had never seriously resumed his studies.

At Cabinet meetings de Valera tried to involve everyone in discussion, which led to very lengthy sessions, whereas the pragmatic Lemass, like Clement Attlee in British politics, used few words and none at all if a grunt or nod would suffice. One Cabinet session a week became the accepted norm and was usually adequate. Survivors of the old guard, Frank Aiken and Seán McEntee, both originally from the North, and Paddy Smith until he resigned as Minister for Agriculture in October 1964, were usually forceful speakers. But while remaining courteous and circumspect, Erskine always held his corner.

One after another of the sacred tenets of Fianna Fáil policy were abandoned during the Lemass years, to the periodic discomfort of older members. Time and again sounds of dissent were stifled by swift action as when Paddy Smith resigned in protest against what he viewed as capitulation to the trade unions. The Cabinet was bound tightly and the party itself was bound by its instinct for survival and tradition of absolute loyalty. This was all Childers had known since he joined in 1932 and he was unable to envisage any other Fianna Fáil. But, not so subtly, traditional dependence on the small man and the rural vote was being equalled by dependence on the generosity of big business. A new bourgeois breed of younger men was thrusting up through the Parliamentary ranks, men more at home in three-piece city suits than bawneen trousers and mentally more attuned to doing business in plush urban surroundings than at a mart or over a farm gate. The populist party was becoming one of privilege. After the general-election victory in April 1965 the Cabinet included Donogh O'Malley at Health, Brian Lenihan at Justice and George Colley at Education. Charles Haughey was now at Agriculture, Neil Blaney at Local Government and Dr Patrick Hillery at Industry and Commerce, having succeeded Jack Lynch who moved to Finance following the retirement of Seán McEntee. Significantly the soft-spoken and affable Jack Lynch was a rising star at the time when Lemass was throwing out hints about retirement, though Lynch steadfastly maintained his disinterest in the leadership.

By the time Lemass finally decided to step down in the autumn of 1966 no obvious successor had emerged and for the first time Fianna Fáil faced a leadership election. The 'succession stakes' fascinated party, press and public alike, but whereas the two latter sectors could only speculate on the merits of the two favourites, George Colley and Charles Haughey, intrigue gripped the Parliamentary party. Squabbles were reported between Colley and O'Malley, a clandestine meeting took place at O'Malley's flat, Boland nominated Blaney, a tough Donegal man, and Lynch eventually agreed to be a candidate for the sake of party unity when pressed by Lemass.

Amidst all the speculation one leading name was conspicuous by its absence. In the raw intrigue of politics Erskine Childers was something of an enigma. A detached, erudite figure, he was essentially a loner in a gregarious profession. Dedicated to his job, sustained by a devoted wife and warm family circle, secure in the knowledge that he was faithfully following parental wishes, he was moved above all else by a desire and concern to serve Ireland to the best of his ability. He needed no lobby to support him, no close circle of disciples to influence one way or another. Never 'one of the boys', he scorned gossip and rarely appeared in the Leinster House bar to socialise. To the younger men he appeared distant. But if his English blood prevented him from getting too close he certainly commanded their respect and never exuded self-importance nor sought to bring all conversations round to himself and his achievements. Sometimes a young deputy paused to chat and came away amazed by his knowledge, though inquisitive strangers found it difficult to penetrate a deep reserve and iron determination not to give himself away. Even close colleagues could meet this reserve at times, but he was always approachable to the extent of continuing to list his private telephone number in the public directory.

In the 1966 vote by the Fianna Fáil Parliamentary Party Erskine Childers was one of the fifty-two deputies who voted for Lynch as leader against nineteen for Colley, Haughey having withdrawn before the contest. The Government settled down under the new Taoiseach though his leadership was under pressure, especially after the failure of the second attempt to replace proportional representation by straight voting at a referendum held in October 1968. Differences were superficially buried but in reality some wounds festered for years to come and the party would later almost be torn apart. The necessary re-shuffle took Haughey to Finance and Colley to Industry and Commerce but the rivalry and distrust which existed between the two men since schooldays was to intensify. Blaney at Agriculture and Boland at Local Goverment shared views not overtly held by others. In 1968 Donogh O'Malley at Education died at the early age of forty-seven having given the country free post-primary schooling and free school transport but having failed to unify the universities in Dublin. Childers gained the Posts and Tele-graphs portfolio in addition to his other responsibilities, together with a Parliamentary Secretary in the person of Patrick Lalor. Under Jack Lynch the policy of direct contact with the Unionists in Northern Ireland was continued and he visited Stormont in December 1967.

Apart from Frank Aiken, who retained the External Affairs portfolio through all the upheavals, Erskine

Childers was now the most senior member of the Government and with two major Departments of State to control his hands were more than full. In addition ripples of unhappiness crossed the domestic scene. One daughter was suddenly and unexpectedly widowed at an early age, left to cope on her own with four youngsters under sixteen. Another daughter was beset by matrimonial problems, and the break-up of his elder son's marriage caused particular distress. An emotional man, such events took their toll and Erskine was beginning to look his age, his face becoming lined and mellowed, the forehead ever more prominent as the hairline receded, the eyes more kindly.

Though he could still work a sixteen-hour day without showing signs of mental or physical fatigue, the Dáil witnessed a rare indication that he was, perhaps, feeling the pace in November 1968 during opposition questions on the decision of B & I to withdraw freight services from Cork. After he had explained the implications of the container revolution in his usual patient, indefatigable manner — regularly so beneficial to Fianna Fáil in defusing explosive situations — the Labour Party leader, Brendan Corish, asked him if he was aware of the inherent difficulties. Looking strangely forlorn Childers replied wearily that he was aware of difficulties occurring everywhere.

The situation in Monaghan constituency, now enlarged to include small parts of Counties Louth and Meath, worried Fianna Fáil as the June 1969 election approached. Assiduous work had been rewarded when Childers polled more first-preference votes than his Fianna Fáil colleague Patrick Mooney in 1965, and with James Dillon safely home Mooney only just beat the second Fine Gael candidate Billy Fox, a Protestant farmer from Ballybay. Fox had since gained prominence as County Secretary of the National Farmers' Association and was expected to attract a large vote from farmers in the Protestant 'Bible belt' of northwest Monaghan. Dillon soon announced his retirement and his mantle had fallen on Senator John Conlan, a well-known member of the County Council. Labour was fighting for the first time and one candidate was a Protestant schoolmaster. Childers could expect little help from Mooney, a reformed smuggler and hard-line Republican, with whom he had coexisted uneasily. Worse still, trouble north of the Border was escalating and many Monaghan people were involved either practically or emotionally.

Events in the North caused increasing alarm after the autumn of 1968. A dispute about the allocation of a local-authority house in Caledon, Co. Tyrone appeared innocuous enough but proved to be the tip of an iceberg which would rend Northern Ireland apart, causing storms in Dublin, London and beyond. Civil Rights marchers, who included some Stormont Nationalist M.P.s, clashed with police in August *en route* from Coalisland to Dungannon and more fiercely in Derry on 5 October when television recorded the brutality of the R.U.C. and viewers saw Gerry Fitt, then Republican Labour M.P. for West Belfast, with blood pouring from a wound in his head caused by a police baton. Battle lines were forming, leading to a withdrawal of the Nationalist opposition from Stormont, further sporadic disturbances throughout the winter and the resignation of Captain O'Neill — branded by the Unionists as a 'Lundy', a leader who was weak enough to talk to the South.

Clearly there were ominous implications for the Dublin Government, and Childers was immediately apprehensive about the effect on tourism as bad news about Ireland regularly hit the headlines. Longer term he was acutely aware that with the imminent retirement of Frank Aiken to the back benches he would be the senior member of a Fianna Fáil Government if he retained his seat and the party won the June 1969 election. It was a sobering thought that as the Northern situation worsened — and there could be little realistic hope of a sudden solution to a problem that had festered for so long — he might well find himself at the centre of the political stage as Ireland was once more engulfed in Civil War. Was history about to repeat itself after an interval of fifty years?

Chapter X
HEALTH — AND
HORROR IN THE NORTH

After leading Fianna Fáil to a substantial and unexpected fourth consecutive general election victory in June 1969, Jack Lynch looked more secure as Taoiseach. A Government re-shuffle, primarily to replace the ageing Frank Aiken and Michael Hilliard who chose the back benches, took Dr Patrick Hillery to External Affairs (renamed Foreign Affairs on 3 March 1971), Brian Lenihan to Transport and Power and Patrick Lalor to Posts and Telegraphs. James Gibbons moved to Defence, Pádraig Faulkner to Education, Seán Flanagan to Lands and by no means least Erskine Childers, now Tánaiste, to Health. Continuity was maintained by George Colley at Industry and Commerce and the seemingly entrenched hard men who brought strong opinions as well as experience to the Cabinet table. Charles Haughey at Finance found a ready affinity with the business sector, while his imaginative gesture in offering tax exemption on earnings to writers, composers, sculptors and painters had caught the world's headlines a few weeks before. At Agriculture Neil Blaney was belligerent yet bland, and Local Government Minister Kevin Boland sometimes lost himself in republican ideology. Rough and often crude, Minister for Justice Micheál O'Mórain appeared to be in declining health. The Cabinet was completed by mild Joseph Brennan at Labour, and younger men such as Gerry Collins, Michael O'Kennedy, Desmond O'Malley and Robert Molloy awaited their chance.

The opposition parties could only benefit from an

infusion of talent. Though it would shortly be rocked by the sudden loss of Gerard Sweetman, tragically killed in a road accident, Fine Gael were ably led by Liam Cosgrave and strengthened by Peter Barry, Richard Burke, John Bruton and Dr Garret Fitzgerald. But the over-all election result had been a disappointment despite conspicuous success in Monaghan, where two Fine Gael deputies were returned for the first time ever, with Erskine Childers only just scratching home ahead of Patrick Mooney as the sole Fianna Fáil deputy. Labour, under Brendan Corish, seemed to be emerging from the shadows with Conor Cruise O'Brien, Dr Noel Browne, Barry Desmond, Justin Keating and David Thornley promising flair and ability.

Steadily escalating upheaval in the North dominated the Nineteenth Dáil from the start and within two months threatened the Fianna Fáil Government by provoking the most serious internal crisis in its history, exposing as never before the dichotomy between rhetoric and reality. With riots and violence engulfing Belfast, Dr Hillery went to London to alert British Foreign Secretary Michael Stewart to the likely consequences if the Apprentice Boys undertook the ritual march around the walls of Derry city on 12 August. As the internal affairs of Northern Ireland had been of no direct interest at Westminster for virtually fifty years Stewart's reluctance to intervene was perhaps understandable but the warning proved timely. Thirty hours of violent street battles ensued as Catholics reacted to provocation and the R.U.C. and sectarian 'B' Special constabulary moved into the Bogside using tear gas on the unprotected populace, resulting in 112 casualties.

Three all-day sessions of a tense and anxious Dublin Cabinet followed in the immediate aftermath and revealed deep divisions among its members, who were torn between what some regarded as a duty to the Northern minority and their responsibility as the elected Government of the Republic. There was unanimity that something must be done for the beleaguered minority and initially a hard-line view from Blaney, Boland and Haughey prevailed. The

Army would be moved up to the Border under the guise of establishing field hospitals for Northern casualties, but Childers, Colley and Hillery cautioned against exacerbating the situation by inflammatory actions and statements: the relative impotence of an Army of some 8000 men with few sophisticated weapons was obvious. Nevertheless, in a radio and television broadcast to the Nation Jack Lynch seemed to reflect a hawkish approach, which was supported at first by Gibbons, Lenihan and Flanagan. After expressing concern and apprehension he continued:

It is evident also, that the Stormont Government is no longer in control of the situation. Indeed the present situation is the inevitable consequence of the policies pursued for decades by successive Stormont Governments. It is clear, also, that the Irish Government can no longer stand by and see innocent people injured and perhaps worse.

It is obvious that the R.U.C. is no longer accepted as an impartial police force. Neither would the employment of British troops be acceptable nor would they be likely to restore peaceful conditions — certainly not in the long term.

The Irish Government has, therefore, requested the British Government to apply immediately to the United Nations for the despatch of a peace-keeping force to the Six Counties of Northern Ireland and have instructed the Irish Permanent Representative to the United Nations to inform the Secretary-General of this request. We have also asked the British Government to see to it that police attacks on the people of Derry should cease immediately.[1]

Promptly and predictably the Northern Premier, Major James Chichester-Clark, described the broadcast as a 'clumsy and intolerable intrusion into our internal affairs', affirming that the 'B' Specials would be used 'to the full', though they were withdrawn from the sensitive areas of Derry only hours afterwards. The spirit of North–South co-operation which highlighted the 'sixties had died ignominiously even before the decade had ended.

With the Army Chief of Staff in attendance on 15 August there is no doubt that the Dublin Cabinet seriously considered invading Derry, Newry and Strabane. But military inadequacy and intervention in Derry by British troops, used for the first time in riot control since partition, led to a rethink by Haughey and Lenihan and, after much persuasion, by Blaney. Boland viewed the change of heart as a rejection of everything Fianna Fáil had ever stood for and stormed out of the meeting after submitting his verbal resignation. Ultimately, after Boland had been in touch with a group of 'volunteers' hoping to go north, President de Valera induced him to withdraw his resignation in the interests of unity, but henceforth Boland confined himself to speaking on departmental matters only. [2]

Protests to the British Government about the use of British troops were abortive and Dr Hillery, apparently briefed by Haughey as well as the Taoiseach, stated Ireland's case for a peace-keeping force to the United Nations Security Council. It was the first time that Ireland, since it became a member of the U.N. in December 1955, had requested a meeting of the Council. The meeting had something of a perfunctory quality and no Irish Government since has asked for mediation on the Irish question. After a meeting with the British Premier, Harold Wilson, soon afterwards, Jack Lynch declared that the Border could not be changed by force and it was his Government's policy to seek reunification by peaceful means, a statement that he repeated on many occasions during the next ten years. But the 'B' Special constabulary was doomed when the Northern Ireland Government accepted the recommendation of the Hunt Committee Report and its duties were taken over by the newly formed Ulster Defence Regiment on 1 April 1970.

An uneasy and superficial normality returned to the Cabinet as Charles Haughey apparently favoured a deal with Britain guaranteeing civil rights in Northern Ireland. Now assuming a central role in the Government approach to the North as a member of the sub-committee set up to administer the Relief Fund to which £100,000 of public funds was later voted, he and Gibbons were also delegated

144

to modernise and re-equip the Army. But whereas Blaney took every opportunity to contradict his leader and the official party policy on the North with apparent impunity, the private papers of Peter Berry, then Secretary to the Department of Justice, reveal that Blaney, Haughey and other Ministers knew of covert attempts to obtain and import arms for the rapidly expanding I.R.A. [3]

The Department of Health, meanwhile, was overtly aware of the brisk energy and penetrating mind of the new Minister. At the helm of a social department for the first time, where the lives and well-being of the Nation were directly influenced, Erskine Childers realised that this might be his final fling. By the next election he would be in his late sixties. Fianna Fáil had already enjoyed power for over a dozen years and an able opposition looked increasingly like a viable alternative Government if the parties could coalesce amicably.

Though he shared the usual male aversion to hospital visiting and was fortunate enough never to have been a patient, medicine and aspects of community health and welfare had always been of interest. His maternal grandfather, Dr Hamilton Osgood of Boston, worked closely with Louis Pasteur, introducing his techniques to the United States, and Erskine himself had early ambitions of choosing medicine as a career, undertaking some preliminary study before switching to history. He took the closest interest in his younger son's medical training. Now, medical journals and papers again featured prominently in his voluminous regular reading. Eminent physicians and leading administrators had to contend with a Minister who not only knew what was going on but could discuss latest trends and ask searching questions about new theories. But if they were kept on their toes his ready understanding was ample compensation and a warm rapport quickly developed with the profession.

Obviously with the Tánaiste as Minister, Health and related matters had a high priority in the Dáil and it was anticipated that financial support would reflect his status.

He was opposed from the start by Dr Noel Browne, who proved a tenacious and persistent questioner although Fine Gael's Deputy Gerard L'Estrange is the best remembered. He lost his cool during a debate on harmful detergents and referred to Erskine Childers as a 'little twerp', which earned him suspension from the House.[4] A couple of years later the Tánaiste called L'Estrange an 'Irish quisling' in a rare outburst, but the hearing of the Ceann Comhairle (Chairman) was found wanting on the second occasion.[5]

Against a background of continuing civil unrest and violence in the North, of refugees fleeing south, and of rumour and suspicion nearer home, Childers was immersed in his Departmental work. Almost daily meetings with hospital committees (about half of which were voluntary or religious boards), doctors, surgeons, nurses and administrators filled his time, and provided a firm base from which to define priorities. In April 1970 Dáil deputies were circulated with a 79-page memorandum giving fundamental information on health problems. More research was urgently required in the areas of heart disease, mental illness and alcoholism, with a need to try to reduce the number of hospital patients and the time they spent there, thus echoing one of the conclusions of the report produced by Professor Patrick Fitzgerald and other members of the Consultative Council on the Reorganisation of Hospital Services.

By February 1970 a major Health Act had been piloted through both Dáil and Senate which precipitated widespread changes and embodied recommendations made in several white papers and reports. A free-choice-of-doctor scheme would benefit less affluent patients and remove at a stroke all social discrimination. The dispensary system was largely replaced and from April 1972 most people could obtain medicine and drugs from retail chemists' shops. Spending on mental health increased dramatically. Eight new Health Boards replaced twenty-seven local health authorities in April 1971. Three Regional Hospital

Boards were set up in Cork, Dublin and Galway to plan and regulate hospital services and a Central Hospital Council was formed in October 1972. Almost as important as the far-reaching statutory changes was a subtle difference in attitude towards the health service. Hospitals tended to be assessed in official terms by the number of patients rather than beds and there was a feeling of care rather than statistics at the very top. Erskine believed that dealing with the sick increased his understanding of people and enabled him, always a good communicator, to communicate even better.

Eight uneasy months for the Cabinet ended in late Spring 1970 when four Ministers and a Parliamentary Secretary left the Government within a few hours. Micheál O'Mórain resigned due to illness on 4 May. Neil Blaney and Charles Haughey were dismissed on 6 May after Liam Cosgrave had passed the Taoiseach information apparently implicating them in unlawful arms importation, an offence with which they were later charged. Kevin Boland together with his Parliamentary Secretary, Paudge Brennan, promptly resigned in sympathy.

As the stability of Government and State was tested more severely than at any time since the Civil War, Jack Lynch appreciated his Tánaiste as never before. A man whose reputation generally was for efficiency and able administration rather than leadership and who was treated almost as a figure of fun by sections of his party demonstrated latent qualities which matched the hour of need. As people everywhere wondered what would happen next speculation mounted. Would the Government fall? Might a coalition be better? A general election seemed imminent as the Fine Gael leader spoke of 'a situation without parallel in the history of this country'. Yet when the dignified demeanour of Erskine Childers appeared on television screens matters assumed a calmer perspective. The most barbed and probing questions were answered directly and unhesitatingly as he sought to reassure viewers that all was under control and it was business as

147

usual for the Government. The *Irish Independent* commented succinctly on his 'Seven Days' performance:

However, the presence of Mr Childers was a steadying influence at a time when rumour was rife and hard information was as scarce as ice cream in hell. In a statesman-like performance he managed to preserve the coolness of a master mariner who knows every trick of the weather. Strange that with his unflappable manner and fluent speech he has not been seen more frequently as a spokesman for his party on television. [6]

In the Dáil Fianna Fáil took a battering as the opposition parties united to attack. For Fine Gael, Richie Ryan mentioned treason and Tom O'Higgins referred to a banana republic. Dr Garret Fitzgerald concentrated his fire on Neil Blaney, describing him as 'a most ruthless, unscrupulous man'. [7] Exposing Fianna Fáil's division, he continued:

I want, at this point, to refer to one man sitting on the opposite benches — the Tánaiste. Neil Blaney's father was sentenced to death; but Erskine Childers's father was executed in the most tragic circumstances. Never by word or deed has this man shown the slightest resentment of those who sent his father to his death. If Neil Blaney were such a man as Erskine Childers, there would be no danger today to the peace of this country. [8]

Childers's own contribution came a week later in a debate on a motion of No Confidence. Using his long experience as a deputy to stress his party's capacity to stand up to violent movements, he utterly rejected the use and support of force to reunify the country.

Nobody in Fianna Fáil who wishes to remain a member of the party can directly or indirectly, officially as a Fianna Fáil person or privately in his own personal capacity, encourage importation of arms into the north, have any contact with illegal organisations in the north, go into the North and inspire armed activity or the use of arms by small individual groups there. That has been made absolutely clear by the Taoiseach already and I want to repeat it here today that anybody who does that is no longer a member of our party. We have made that clear beyond all doubt.

Nobody can remain a member of Fianna Fáil who is not aware of the reality of the situation in the North as outlined by the Taoiseach.

Whether we like it or not the British Army is in control of public order in the North and any military intervention, official or unofficial by armed illegal groups or by anybody, that does not take account of the official position of the British Army there, would be to invite a worse position should rioting break out and would be completely insane, in fact, both from a political and a military point of view or even from the point of view of saving human life. These are the realities we face in our party and any person who is a member of Fianna Fáil is bound to accept these realities and understand that military intervention of this kind might bring far worse disaster to the minority in the North than they could possibly conceive.[9]

The public-school ethos and strict moral code absorbed from his parents remained with Erskine Childers all his life. As a deputy and Minister he was a dedicated professional, yet there was a diffidence, a sort of detachment from the factional side of politics. Never active in the party hierarchy, he lacked the feel of a native Irishman for certain situations. Colleagues tolerated memoranda from him about their Departments with amusement if not equanimity. He rarely expressed dislike of individuals or even denounced individual opponents, and never stooped to intrigue.

If things changed for Fianna Fáil after what is always referred to as the Arms Crisis, the same was certainly true for Childers. His antipathy to Blaney and Haughey, both of whom he had viewed through increasingly jaundiced eyes for some time, became public knowledge. In July 1970 he became Vice-President of Fianna Fáil as Jack Lynch strengthened the party structure. In a Cabinet which now included four new, young and inexperienced Ministers (see page 151) and over which Jack Lynch presided with greater command than at any time hitherto, he became more assertive. At home and abroad he shouldered more of the burden of stating Ireland's case for peace.

Constituency affairs were never neglected though visits to Monaghan now tended to be shorter. Childers usually raced north on a Monday afternoon to hold a surgery prior to addressing an evening meeting. A light was fitted under the dashboard of his Mercedes Benz so that he could sit beside the driver and read or study papers when returning home through the night. It was essential to keep in the closest personal touch with an area where happenings North of the Border impinged more directly than almost anywhere else. A substantial section of the rank-and-file Fianna Fáil membership identified closely with the Northern minority even if they did not wholly condone the methods of the Provisional I.R.A. The local newspaper, the *Northern Standard*, took a hawkish stance and appeared at times to support the men of violence, while former Deputy Paddy Mooney was clearly sore at losing his seat having polled more first-preference votes than Childers.

Mooney supported formation of a local Civil Rights Association in August 1969 and made calls for the Irish Peace Keeping contingent to be withdrawn from Cyprus and redeployed in the North. Though remaining within the party he frequently met Neil Blaney as the Donegal Deputy travelled across Monaghan to and from Dublin. When Jack Lynch spoke in the constituency sometime later Mooney was prominent. 'Howya', he greeted Rita Childers; 'And the cock crowed thrice', growled Paddy Smith, the veteran Cavan Deputy who was standing near by.

Childers's courage in consistently and unequivocally condemning violence in such sensitive circumstances was recognised by his Protestant constituents as well as by the majority of Catholics. Week after week he clashed with the *Northern Standard*, telling the Editor 'your issue this week is full of extreme propaganda, please correct this by publishing the enclosed [letter]'.[10] Slowly the local Fianna Fáil organisation divided into pro-Childers branches and those which took a 'hawkish' view of contemporary events.

A close rapport was established with the Church of

THE FIANNA FÁIL CABINET 1969 TO 1973

	Before 8 May 1970	After 8 May 1970
Taoiseach	Jack Lynch	
Tánaiste and Health	Erskine H. Childers	
External Affairs (Foreign Affairs from 3 March 1971)	Dr Patrick Hillery	(Brian Lenihan from January 1973)
Finance	Charles J. Haughey	George Colley†
Industry and Commerce	George Colley†	Patrick Lalor
Agriculture and Fisheries	Neil Blaney	James Gibbons
Local Government	Kevin Boland*	Robert Molloy
Defence	James Gibbons	Jeremiah Cronin
Justice	Micheál O'Mórain	Desmond O'Malley
Posts and Telegraphs	Patrick Lalor	Gerard Collins
Education	Pádraig Faulkner	
Transport and Power	Brian Lenihan	(Michael O'Kennedy from January 1973)
Labour and Social Welfare	Joseph Brennan*	
Lands	Seán Flanagan	

†Also responsible for the Gaeltacht.
*Responsibility for Social Welfare was combined with Local Government before 8 May 1970 and with Labour thereafter.

Ireland Rector of Monaghan town, Archdeacon Heavener, who was also Chairman of the Protestant Association and later became Bishop of Clogher. Bishop Heavener regards Erskine Childers as a statesman rather than a politician and believes that no other man of any party or denomination did so much to lift Ireland out of the morass into which it had fallen through the agony of revolution and civil war. But Desmond O'Malley sometimes thought his Tánaiste put too much store on what his Protestant constituents thought. As Minister for Justice he recalls receiving regular telephone calls on Tuesday mornings about an hour before the Cabinet met and having to consistently reassure

Childers that everything possible was being done to protect Border areas from I.R.A. training squads and fugitives. Even production of documentary proof that military training took place north rather than south of the Border did not entirely appease him.

Disharmony in Monaghan, dissent within the party and the challenge of the Health portfolio were almost all-absorbing. But not quite, for Ireland was preparing to take what the Taoiseach described as 'the most momentous step taken by the Irish people since the foundation of the State'.[11] Membership of the European Economic Community, unsuccessfully sought in 1961 and 1967, now seemed a realistic prospect following the retirement of General de Gaulle in April 1969 and a consequent lessening of French objections to British entry. Denmark and Norway in addition to Ireland and Britain anticipated opening negotiations with the six. Dr Hillery visited his European counterparts, and preliminary talks had been held in London before the Dáil debated the implications following a white paper.

For Erskine Childers this was the realisation of a long-held vision. A passionate believer in national distinctiveness as a young man, he had rejected the concept of narrow, isolated nationalism. Far from reducing sovereignty he realised that membership would lessen dependence on one trading partner and make Ireland an equal partner with other Western European countries. As time passed and tariffs were broken down, many problems associated with the Border would begin to disappear. Europe was as remote as Outer Mongolia for some Dáil deputies, and Childers was one of the few who not only had a good grasp of its geography and history but practical experience of life on the Continent. In June 1970, not long after the end of a stormy Parliamentary Party meeting which echoed with dated, sterile arguments about coercing Northern Protestants, the Tánaiste was waxing almost lyrical about fresh horizons:

I believe our joining the E.E.C. will immensely enrich our national identity, much of which is partly concealed. Our close contact with nations with different cultures and languages, our visiting them, negotiating with them and collaborating with them will be of immense value in stimulating the Irish personality.

We have survived through centuries because of our capacity for adaptability and for our tenacity in facing appallingly difficult situations and in facing the effects of oppression over a long period. We have for too long negotiated and traded with just one partner. It will be of immense benefit to us to have to get to know other people, to work and collaborate with them, to argue with them and defend ourselves when our interests are challenged.

We have had this utter dependence on Britain for no other reason than our geographical position. However, with modern communications and with our opportunity to join the E.E.C. we will be able to come closer to the dynamic world of the German people. Our connection with those nations of the E.E.C. who speak the Latin tongue will be magnificent for the Irish personality. Although I am only partly Irish, whenever I have been in France I have felt far nearer in temperament to the French people than I do to the people of any other country. This may be a purely personal impression but the fact that we shall have to learn to understand the personality of the French and Italian peoples, to learn their weaknesses and their strength, will be of immense value in strengthening that part of the Irish personality that has not been overlaid with the English influence.

At the same time we will have to demonstrate our own identity. If we are going to survive in Europe far more Irish people will have to identify themselves as Irish. We have never had to do this much with Great Britain, we simply had to trade there. When we go into Europe each of us must know enough about our country to demonstrate his identity and that in itself will be a useful exercise for many people who have failed to learn enough about our cultural heritage or even what constitutes the Irish economy. As ambassadors in Europe we must have far more understanding of what is best in Ireland, of the things we produce, of our literature and of our culture. That will also be a stimulus to our development as a nation.

Towards the conclusion he turned to the question of Northern Ireland:

I have met people in the North who, even though they continue to say they are Unionists, admit that in the field of European collaboration, European negotiation and the growth of European federation, it would be a good thing from their standpoint if they could feel they were part of a negotiating team in which their interests would get full consideration and full examination rather than that they should be involved inevitably in the massive agenda from month to month and year to year of the British Board of Trade.[12]

Forty-eight hours after his testimony of faith in a European future, Erskine's thoughts were brought closer to home. Together with Robert Barton he took part in an hour-long programme, 'I Die Loving England', about his father and broadcast by the B.B.C. on Radio 4 to mark the centenary of his birth. A re-examination of the elder Erskine's brief and enigmatic part in Irish history was inevitable and major articles in two Dublin newspapers helped to stimulate interest. A Memorial Committee was established soon afterwards in County Wicklow and henceforth organised a parade to the Republican Plot in Glasnevin Cemetery each November as well as providing a bursary in Marine Biology tenable at University College, Galway. Most gratifying of all to his son had been a public tribute from Harold Wilson during the course of a St Patrick's night banquet in Liverpool.

After half a century positive memories of his father were mostly blurred almost beyond recognition. Asked what he was really like the answer was disarmingly frank: 'I am waiting to read Andrew's book in order to find out.' Andrew Boyle had been commissioned to write the authorised biography once the elder Erskine's personal papers were available and Erskine was busily compiling a bibliography of works which Boyle might usefully consult. It was a task he enjoyed hugely and often tackled in the small hours at the end of a 16-hour working-day.

But the spectre of civil war, always alluded to as the most terrible of all conflicts, continually haunted Childers as Irishmen shot each other for political reasons. He spoke out fearlessly in the cause of peace and settlement by negotiation and agreement. At home he expressed his views forcefully in a marathon North–South television debate with Brian Faulkner. In Britain, the Oxford Union was the forum for debate on the motion 'That this House would welcome the re-unification of Ireland' and Erskine carried on the discussion virtually all night back at the hotel where he and Stormont M.P. Roy Bradford were staying. Further afield he spoke on French television and at St Louis, Missouri, where he attacked both British policy and the I.R.A. Media appearances outnumbered those of the Taoiseach at this period and the newly found prominence and value to the Nation was acknowledged when *News Week* magazine named him 'Minister of the Year' for 1970.

Speeches strongly critical of the I.R.A. were not popular in some quarters and events such as the introduction of internment in the North in August 1971 and Bloody Sunday in January 1972, when thirteen people were shot dead in Derry, caused waves of revulsion to sweep the country. At Trinity College, Dublin, heckling and interruptions forced a premature end to at least one address. Taunts of 'Imperialist tool' greeted him elsewhere. Despite omnipresent detectives, danger was real. Mrs Rita Childers retains vivid recollections of a conversation about kidnapping during a train journey from Salisbury to Waterloo. With a pained expression Erskine said quietly and deliberately, 'If it happened to you, we couldn't give in. I could never agree to a ransom demand.'

A Mediterranean cruise in late summer 1971 proved less than therapeutic. Erskine was near to exhaustion, and the first couple of days aboard the liner bound for Naples, Corfu and North Africa were comfortably restful. Soon the novelty of relaxing gave way to frustration at the lack of news and the family listened to speculation about what might be happening at home. Finally boredom manifested itself in a silent contempt for those fellow passengers who contentedly lazed on deck all day with nothing to occupy their minds other than contemplation of the evening's entertainment. Back at Southampton the Childers family were the first to disembark as an anxious Tánaiste learned that Jack Lynch and Brian Faulkner, now Stormont Premier, had both been invited to Chequers by Edward Heath for the first Tripartite Talks since 1925.

Having failed to capitalise on Fianna Fáil's difficulties in the immediate aftermath of the arms crisis, the opposition kept up the pressure in the Dáil. Blaney was acquitted of all criminal charges at a preliminary hearing in July 1970 but Haughey and three others stood trial at the Four Courts in September and October. The first trial was stopped after allegations about its unfair tone, but all four defendants were found not guilty on the fourteenth day of the second trial, following which Haughey challenged Lynch to resign. The Government and Lynch survived a second confidence motion with the support of Haughey and Blaney in November 1970, but the mercurial Boland resigned his Dáil seat fifteen minutes before the end of the debate and stormed from the House. His bitterness at what he interpreted as the party turning its back on its primary reason for existing ran too deep, and he broke away to found the ill-conceived Aontacht Éireann Party which soon faded.

The role of James Gibbons in the arms affair came under close scrutiny and is more difficult to determine. As Minister for Defence he was certainly closely associated with Haughey after August 1969. His evidence conflicted with Haughey's and each contradicted the sworn testimony of the other, adding a further Gilbertian twist to the bizarre episode. But Gibbons was promoted to become Minister for Agriculture, later revealing to the Public Accounts Committee that money from the Government's Distress Fund had in fact been used for the attempted import of arms. This was in contradiction to the Taoiseach's assurance given to the Dáil that no State funds were involved. Fine Gael smelt blood and after an abortive attempt in April, Liam Cosgrave eventually moved a

Censure Motion on the Agriculture Minister in November 1971. Taunted by Conor Cruise O'Brien about his integrity, Erskine Childers was soon on his feet:

I have had experience of Government, some seventeen years in all, and of being associated with a great many Ministers. Like other Ministers I was, naturally, shocked by the events of April 1970, but I wish to say that at no time did I have reason to believe that the former Minister for Defence, Deputy Gibbons, was concerned, directly or indirectly, with the smuggling of arms into the North. Ultimately this is a question of human faith. I believe Deputy Jim Gibbons. I do not believe those who gave evidence which suggested that he had complicity in this matter and I think that everything Deputy Gibbons said in regard to the later action of these persons is of importance in this matter.[13]

At the end of a debate, which proved to be the parting of the ways for the dissidents, Fianna Fáil won the division by three votes. Neil Blaney and Paudge Brennan abstained and were forthwith expelled from the Parliamentary Party. Their contempt for the leadership was blatant and it was no coincidence that the 1971 Health Regulations Bill only scraped through by one vote whilst they were inexplicably absent.[14] Charles Haughey voted with the Government, thus taking another positive step towards rehabilitating himself within Fianna Fáil. After the opportunist challenge in the wake of his acquittal Haughey turned quietly to the grassroots of the Party and tirelessly stomped the country to meet and address the local cumainn (branches), rapidly becoming a favourite with local officials and rank-and-file members. This groundwork was to prove the base from which he would launch his successful campaign for leadership of the Party.

In the first three months of 1972 Erskine Childers was the leading Fianna Fáil speaker in the Dáil with 8,969 lines of print in the official reports against 12,130 by Dr Garret Fitzgerald of Fine Gael and 10,629 by Labour Deputy James Tully. But his most eloquent moment was a silent one. As Charles Haughey walked on to the platform at the Fianna

Fáil Ard Fheis (Annual Conference) in February, greeted by the Party hierarchy after his election as a Vice-President, Childers sat silently reading his newspaper. He was dismayed at the prospect of Haughey again ingratiating himself and was unwilling to compromise in any way, constantly urging Jack Lynch never to restore him to any prominence in the Parliamentary Party. There could be no fudging of the issue and no half measures. As a constituent had once complained when he declined to give her daughter preferential treatment in obtaining a Post Office job, he was incapable of 'putting a face on it'. Nor, it transpired subsequently, could Frank Aiken. After Haughey was ratified as a Fianna Fáil candidate at the 1973 general election, he declined to contest the Louth seat which he had held for fifty years. It appears that other senior figures harboured similar misgivings, including Paddy Smith, but the tradition of loyalty and a reluctance to 'rock the boat' prevented any concerted action.[15]

A further meeting, and a highly distasteful one, took place between Kevin Boland and some of his erstwhile Fianna Fáil colleagues. At the funeral of his father, Gerald Boland, in January 1973 Erskine Childers was accompanied by Brian Lenihan and Patrick Lalor to the Dominican Church in Dublin. Members of the Boland family endeavoured to prevent them from entering but as he was representing the Taoiseach Childers was eventually shown to the *prie dieu*, later being forced to move to the back of the church. Kevin Boland stated openly that 'traitors, perjurers and Free Staters' were not welcome at the Requiem Mass and Childers told the press that it was the first time in his life that such an incident had taken place; even after the Civil War when there was great bitterness on both sides nothing remotely similar had occurred.[16]

Controversy continues to surround people and money involved in what was assuredly an attempt to import arms into Ireland. The Public Accounts Committee was authorised by the Dáil on 1 December 1970 to investigate the circumstances surrounding the spending of the

£100,000 grant-in-aid to the Northern Ireland Relief Fund. It sat intermittently over an eighteen-month period and eventually concluded that nearly half of the money had not been used for the purposes intended by the Dáil. Early in 1977 the Coalition Government commenced legal proceedings in Hamburg for the recovery of more than £20,000 from a West German arms dealer, but the attempt proved abortive when a lawsuit was dismissed a year later without a word of explanation. Fianna Fáil were by then back in power and George Colley, who had resumed office as Minister for Finance, announced that the Government had decided to drop its attempt to recover any money. But numerous questions remain unanswered about the whole affair.

Though he was only one of thousands who cared deeply about deterioration in aspects of national life, Erskine Childers appreciated more clearly than most the contradictions and ambivalence in attitudes towards the neighbouring island. Irish mistrust of British intentions over the long period of British rule combined with nationalist resentment at the partition of the island meant that anti-British sentiment still lingered on in contrast to a genuinely warm welcome for British visitors and an acknowledgment that Irishmen have continued to enjoy a chance to earn a living across the water when their own country has failed them.

Increasing prosperity was doing more to anglicise Ireland in some respects than centuries of British rule. As the 'English' disease struck it prompted a distinctly 'English' response. Soulless new towns and suburbs spawned high-rise flats and social problems so that Ballymun, Kilbarrack and Tallaght are interchangeable with Basildon, Kirkby and Telford. Demolition of graceful Georgian houses in city and town centres to make way for ubiquitous concrete-and-glass office blocks endangered a proud architectural heritage. Shopping centres dealt mortal blows at small traders, whilst slack or suspect planning committees allowed gaudy signs to sprout irregularly from shops and bars. Urban communities began to look more and more like their British counterparts. Industrial disputes and inter-union squabbles continually threatened public services and usually seemed more protracted than British strikes. In contrast to the fact that Ireland is a conservative country holding firmly to traditional values, Anglo-American sub-culture, aided and abetted by television, was taking a firm hold and drug taking, armed robbery, gang warfare, and sexual abuse were all on the increase.

Against such a background Erskine Childers was the most prominent and persistently persuasive voice raised in defence of a distinctive Irish character. An article, 'The Ireland I Love', written for *The Tablet* in March 1972 might almost be regarded as his *De Profundis*.

I love this island where the horrors of urban anonymity of living, the horrors of excessive pollution and gross overcrowding are limited. I love living in a country where everyone, however inadequately, feels compassion for someone else: where excessive individualism is attenuated by a religious sense of being on a pilgrimage; where people love to talk even if in spiralling inconsequential measure. I love living in a community where it is possible for every citizen to feel a sense of responsibility for those living in his neighbourhood.

I love living in a country where without excessive, maddening inefficiency, the rat race is only beginning in some areas of living. I love being able to send my child to almost any school, knowing that as I prepare the child to face adolescence the child will not be corrupted by foul influences.

I find the near proximity, the pervasive influence of clergy and nuns of all denominations absolutely essential if we are to escape the virtual obliteration of individual and collective responsibility for the state of society.

I revel in the moderate, rainy climate which, please God, will keep away the jet sets and hoards of package trippers basking on sunsoaked beaches. I enjoy a society which is in one way class conscious but where in a few minutes of talking or convening at a meeting the class consciousness vanishes.

I regard the Unionists of the North as contributing instrumentalists in a national orchestra where the musical cadence is Irish but the musicians are all of very mixed racial origin and the music is composed of many melodic components. The southern sounds by themselves need enlivening while the northern tune needs the touch of the South.

I must state unequivocally that since I have been a Protestant Member of Parliament the number of alleged acts of discrimination reported to me against Protestants has been negligible. Since the coming of Pope John XXIII the very rare and local highly publicised acts of bigotry have vanished. The Protestants publicly avow the full opportunity for life they have enjoyed since 1921.

Soon afterwards at Kilkenny he repeated that no inducement on earth would ever make him exchange life in Ireland for life in a State where religion counted for little. Ireland, he said, 'was the happiest place in the world to live in for almost all the people here', and his greatest personal ambition was to contribute in some way to preventing Ireland from reaching a stage where the adverse effects of the affluent society destroyed everything gained in creating equality of opportunity.[17]

Inconsistency in espousing and promoting the causes which he adopted as his own was the very last thing of which Erskine Childers could be accused. Encouraging national self-confidence had, perhaps, given way over the years to urging retention of national distinctiveness but the ambivalence and ambiguity of outlook remained an ongoing theme of speeches. Also characteristic were the familiar economic speeches in the Dáil using comparative statistics from other countries to demonstrate Ireland's success or otherwise in various spheres, up-dated regularly over thirty years or more, and as relevant in 1971 (when Labour Deputy Frank Cluskey said such a speech had been written five years before![18]) as in 1941. As Minister for Health he constantly warned of the dangers of excessive drinking and smoking, despite the fact that he personally enjoyed alcoholic refreshment in moderation and was seldom seen without his pipe. The Irish Society for the Prevention of Cruelty to Children were told that he regarded alcoholism as the 'greatest single scourge' in the country and he ordered a survey to publicise the 'shattering facts'.

The debilitating effects of continuous bad news from the media was another oft-repeated topic expanded in appropriate circumstances. At a symposium on 'Mass Communications in Contemporary Society' at University College, Dublin in December 1971 delegates learned that the press, radio and television could contract the length of bad news without reducing the impact and challenge implied to those in authority, without omitting any items. The space could then be used to describe the effort being made by international agencies, the Churches, Governments and peoples to solve their problems and advance a better civilisation.

Speeches about 'the rounds system of drink buying' and 'good news' made excellent copy and they were reported with implied suggestions of 'bee in bonnet' crankiness. The temptation to ridicule someone who was different or not quite understood was irresistible, yet affectionate rather than malicious. Media hilarity boiled over when Erskine mistakenly approached Fianna Fáil Senator Mark Killilea for a pair (a Parliamentary term for two opposed members who agree not to vote on a specific motion, often because they will be absent from the House) and then exacerbated the situation by writing a serious letter of explanation to *The Irish Times*. [19] At about the same time an apocryphal story circulating in Leinster House suggested that imminent E.E.C. membership had given fresh impetus to the quest for comparative statistics. Reading, as so often, far into the night he reportedly awoke his wife at about 3 a.m. to inform her that a Baltic herring contained on average 10 per cent less fat than an Irish herring!

Ireland together with Britain, Denmark and Norway signed a Treaty of Accession to the European Economic Community in the Palais d'Egmont, Brussels on 22 January 1972 at a ceremony that was delayed for an hour because the British Prime Minister, Edward Heath, was assaulted as he entered the building. Though Norwegian plans were ultimately thwarted by the populace, the people of Ireland voted in favour by a majority of almost five to one in a referendum on 10 May 1972. There was some speculation that Erskine Childers might become his country's first Commissioner in Brussels and he was approached to this end by some high-ranking E.E.C. officials. Few in Ireland were more suited. His broad culture, knowledge of European history and geography, fluent French, capacity for hard work and enthusiasm for the concept were unquestioned, and his prestige as a Deputy Prime Minister would have given him considerable influence. But Jack Lynch would not hear of the idea. Loss of his right-hand man might well have caused more instability in the Government, and a by-election defeat in Monaghan could not be ruled out.

Dr Patrick Hillery was appointed Commissioner in September 1972 and took up his office when Irish membership became effective on 1 January 1973. Later that month Erskine and Rita Childers went to London as guests of Sir Robert Mayer for a 'Fanfare for Europe Concert' at the Royal Festival Hall to celebrate the enlarged E.E.C. Though he was not listed as a speaker at the subsequent reception at the Savoy, Erskine made some impromptu remarks which were much appreciated, especially his point that the title should be the European Cultural Community as economics was such a contentious subject.

Despite the grim background of continuing violence in Northern Ireland, security problems in the Republic and dissension just beneath the surface in the Fianna Fáil party, there were times of great personal pleasure for Erskine during his years as Tánaiste. Artistic occasions were such, and at the Robertstown Canal Fiesta in Co. Kildare and in St Patrick's Cathedral he had opportunities to read from his grandmother's anthology, *City without Walls*. At the Irish Embassy in London in May 1970 he launched an eighteen-volume edition of Lady Gregory's complete

163

works and in August 1972 he returned to Sligo to open the Thirteenth Yeats International Summer School. Linking the poet to contemporary problems he appealed to all impatient, violent men, oppressors and the bitter, to read Yeats beside the lake and find some enchantment to deter them from their unprofitable strife. 'Preserve that which is living', he said, 'and help the two Irelands, Gaelic and Anglo, so to unite that neither shall shed its pride.'[20]

Erskine never neglected his English links. Through the years Gresham's School was kept advised of his progress and he usually attended reunions of his 'year' at Cambridge. The Master of Trinity College, Lord (R. A.) Butler, wrote personally to invite him in June 1972 and he sat next to the British statesman at table. Even more unexpected was an invitation to partake in a ceremony in Pontefract, Yorkshire commemorating the centenary of the introduction of the secret ballot in Britain. The journey was essentially an exercise in family piety as Hugh Childers, the erstwhile Chancellor of the Exchequer, had successfully fought the Pontefract by-election in August 1872 against the Conservative Lord Pollington. At the ceremony both Erskine and the Earl of Mexborough spoke and recalled what they knew of their ancestors.

The Fianna Fáil Government entered its sixteenth consecutive year in office in 1972 and only the Taoiseach, Jack Lynch, and Tánaiste, Erskine Childers, had served throughout as full members. Some people felt that the latter, older by over eleven years, would never realise his erstwhile ambition to become his country's Prime Minister. He had missed the chance of going to Brussels as Irish Commissioner. The Irish Presidency would fall vacant in 1973 upon the retirement of Mr de Valera but, although Erskine's name was occasionally mentioned as a possible candidate, the same applied to several others; and after his impressive campaign in 1966, when he only lost by 10,568 votes from a total of over 1.1m. cast, Tom O'Higgins of Fine Gael was a clear favourite. At the end of the day the best hope seemed to be a Fianna Fáil victory in the next election so that he could continue his work at Health, which he found challenging and rewarding. But with Fine Gael and Labour likely to fight as a National Coalition, such a victory was far from certain despite the personal popularity of Jack Lynch and the enhanced reputation of Erskine Childers.

Chapter XI
A RELUCTANT CANDIDATE

At the start of 1973 serious consideration of a Presidential candidate could no longer be postponed by Fianna Fáil despite recent preoccupation with law and order after explosions in Dublin, the arrest of Provisional I.R.A. Chief of Staff, Seán MacStoifáin and the dismissal of the R.T.E. Authority for permitting an interview with MacStiofáin to be transmitted. With Fine Gael's Tom O'Higgins waiting in the wings since 1966 it was late, many thought too late, unless Jack Lynch could be persuaded to run. Names frequently mentioned included Frank Aiken, senior member of the Parliamentary party, Michael Yeats, son of W. B. Yeats and Chairman of the Seanad, and Erskine Childers.

Best-known names internationally were Yeats and Childers. Both were English-born Protestants, important in an ecumenical and North–South context. Whereas Yeats was the younger by 15 years, his outspoken republicanism, which even at St Columba's College is said to have repulsed Brian Faulkner, and the fact that he was a less accomplished politician rendered him not so acceptable. Though 'a name', he was not well known personally in the country and lacked a public image. There was talk of an agreed candidate. Lord O'Neill of the Maine was one kite flown by Fianna Fáil, and leaders of the three parties met towards the end of January 1973. With Mr Lynch adamant that he would not stand, Childers began to look the odds-on choice if Fianna Fáil had to field a candidate.

The Tánaiste, however, had other ideas and felt it opportune to say so. He was thoroughly enjoying the Health portfolio where his work was far from finished. In good physical shape for his years he still relished the cut and thrust of political life, particularly the opportunity to translate ideas and policies into actions. The thought of a passive role where he would clearly be constrained was in some respects anathema and on 25 January 1973 the press was advised that under no circumstances would he allow his name to go forward.

Inter-party talks never seriously got off the ground. Fianna Fáil could never support Tom O'Higgins as an agreed candidate and Fine Gael would have no other. He was formally selected on 31 January, whereupon Jack Lynch moved quickly. On 5 February dissolution of the Nineteenth Dáil was announced and a general election called for 28 February. The decision caught the country unawares but enabled Lynch to launch his campaign on B.B.C. television's 'Panorama' programme the same evening, when he called on the British Government to outlaw the U.D.A. The great hope was a victory to sweep a Fianna Fáil candidate into the Presidency in its wake or at worst to cushion the blow of O'Higgins's success.

Heavy snow carpeted the fields of Monaghan as Childers prepared to contest the seat for the fourth time. Even after a dozen years he was far from entrenched and the 1969 result had been too close for comfort. But the party machine was busy in the area on his behalf and at a constituency convention at Castleblayney on 11 February, chaired by Paddy Smith, he was selected unanimously whereas Patrick Mooney who polled the highest number of Fianna Fáil first-preference votes in 1969 was dropped. James Leonard, a native of Smithborough and manager of the agricultural section of Monaghan co-operative, who had been Erskine's election agent, was selected in his place. The affronted Mooney, unashamed associate of Neil Blaney, stalked out of the hall announcing his intention of running as an independent. Ultimately the field comprised eight candidates, including John Conlan and Billy Fox, seeking re-election for Fine Gael, and Patrick Turley, Editor of the *Northern Standard*, running on an Independent Unity label.

Like many Fianna Fáil colleagues Childers concentrated much verbal fire during the campaign on the apparently tenuous nature of the Fine Gael–Labour coalition. At Stonetown, County Louth, on 20 February he pointed to divisions within the Labour Party suggesting that a Labour base for Fine Gael was uncertain and unreliable. Fianna Fáil's record, particularly on law-and-order measures such as the Forcible Entry and Offences against the State Acts, was defended strongly.[1] Five days later at Inniskeen, the village famous as the home of Patrick Kavanagh the poet, he warned that the left wing of the coalition would try to bleed better-off citizens, and that this would lead to emigration of professional people.[2] Childers fought a strong campaign, remaining in Monaghan for most of the time and taking no chances.

Though there were indications that the Protestant Association vote might not be so strongly behind Billy Fox as in 1969, it was a genuine surprise for Childers to find himself elected at the first count with a staggering 2,356 votes more than Conlan, who had to wait until the fifth count, whilst at the sixth Leonard was 720 votes ahead of Fox. Fianna Fáil thus regained the second seat. Mooney was badly beaten and joined Aontacht Éireann shortly afterwards before sliding quietly into obscurity.

Despite regaining a second Monaghan seat, the result nationally brought the first change of Government in Ireland for sixteen years. When the last votes were counted Fianna Fáil had sixty-nine deputies, Fine Gael fifty-four, Labour nineteen, and there were two Independents. Leading casualty was Foreign Affairs Minister, Brian Lenihan. Neil Blaney and Charles Haughey headed their respective polls with large majorities but the other leading dissident, Kevin Boland, was thrashed. National Coalition Taoiseach, Liam Cosgrave, appointed Labour leader Brendan Corish to be Tánaiste, and Minister for Health and Childers was out of a job overnight. However he prepared a long memorandum about the Department for his successor and Corish went out of his way to thank him.

Tom O'Higgins had not contested the general election and the coalition success ensured that Labour would not field a Presidential candidate against him.

Having taken the personal decision not to stand, Mr Lynch realised that Erskine Childers represented the only serious hope of a Fianna Fáil Presidential victory, and after consulting Paddy Smith, senior member of the Parliamentary Party, he personally asked him to reconsider.[3] Such a request from the party leader could not lightly be rejected. Whichever way the question was approached, in the final analysis there was only one answer. Personal considerations must take second place. Ireland must come first. Irish Presidential elections are hardly calculated to excite the populace whose lives are not influenced in any real sense by the result. No philosophies or policies are at stake and the choice is essentially between the personalities involved. Nevertheless the chances for an individual are negligible without political backing. In 1973 the prestige of government and opposition parties was at stake, especially that of Fianna Fáil, smarting under a general-election defeat for only the fifth time in its history.

The role of the Head of State is clearly defined in Article 13(9) of the 1937 Constitution and there is a strict limit even on the way that this can be interpreted without Government approval. Nevertheless when Childers told Lynch that he was prepared to run he made it a condition that the role of the President should be expanded and used to greater effect. Neither the Fianna Fáil Parliamentary party nor the National Executive demurred and his candidacy was officially announced on 6 April, by which time 30 May had been named as polling day. At his press conference Childers, typically, sought to draw an artistic parallel to illustrate a broader Presidency. He envisaged looking to the future, by displaying a series of paintings depicting the advance of the nation and of the problems to be solved.

Look at these pictures, think about them, see how they conform with your own idea of what Ireland should be like in ten or

169

twenty years' time. Discuss the ideas in these pictures with your organisation, your political party.

He gave his view that the recommendations of the second Vatican Council pointed the way and unless these were taken seriously Ireland would become like any other North European country.

Inevitably, religion figured among the questions which he faced. Childers said he had never used the fact that he was a Protestant to advance any cause and with regard to the North saw no reason why a President could not speak about reconciliation, the agreed policy of all Dáil parties. He envisaged people from all sides meeting at Áras an Uachtaráin to talk together. Interest in youth was emphasised and all possible encouragement would be given to young people's organisations.

Strong echoes of the Civil War were evoked by the prospect of a contest between Childers and O'Higgins, two of the most famous names in twentieth-century Irish history. The O'Higgins family were as steeped in politics as the Childerses, having taken the Free State side and subsequently worked always in the Cumann na Gaedheal/ Fine Gael interest. In earlier times the candidate's great-grandfather, T. D. O'Sullivan, had sat at Westminster as Nationalist member for West Donegal. There was a strong medical background and Tom O'Higgins had been Minister for Health between 1954 and 1957. Tragedy too, had struck. The Presidential candidate's grandfather, Dr Thomas O'Higgins of Stradbally, Co. Laois, was shot dead at his home by republicans in February 1923 and his Uncle Kevin, Minister of Home Affairs in the first Free State Government and signatory of the elder Erskine's death warrant, was assassinated in the street near his home at Booterstown in July 1927. The candidate's father, Dr T. F. O'Higgins was a Dáil deputy for twenty-five years and Minister for Defence in the first Inter-Party Government and his brother Michael was a member of the Seanad.

Tom O'Higgins was born at Sunday's Well, Cork in 1916

and educated at Clongowes, the Jesuit College near Naas, County Kildare before reading Law at University College, Dublin. In the Dáil he represented Laois–Offaly from 1948 to 1969 and South County Dublin from then until February 1973. During the long years in opposition he developed a thriving Bar practice and also helped to reshape Fine Gael in the 'Just Society' movement of the 1960s. The 1966 Presidential campaign revealed him for the first time as a man of vision, speaking clearly on many issues including the then peaceful North. Ever since he had been regarded as favourite for the Presidency, and Fine Gael morale and confidence were never higher than in mid-April 1973 when his countrywide campaign got under way with a rally at Stradbally.

By contrast Fianna Fáil spent the whole of April carefully planning behind the scenes, and not until a May Day press conference at Leinster House was the strategy unveiled. With his unusual background Childers could legitimately campaign under the banner of 'A President for all the Nation'. The candidate had kept himself in the public eye, events such as the award of an honorary Doctor of Laws degree by the National University on 12 April providing unsought yet welcome publicity. Photographs at Iveagh House with the Chancellor, President de Valera, and other distinguished recipients could only help.

Fianna Fáil campaign plans provided for a 3,000-mile countrywide tour visiting virtually every county. Childers said at the time, if anyone had told him a year before that he would spend much of late spring 1973 touring Ireland by bus he'd have told them they were mad. George Colley directed operations, with Brian Lenihan co-ordinating from Dublin. Local organisation in fourteen regions was handled by former ministers or parliamentary secretaries. Seated next to Jack Lynch at the press briefing Childers developed his ideas for expanding the Presidency, envisaging himself as both composer and conductor of the national orchestra. He declared that he felt like an ordinary hill-walker climbing an unexplored mountain and hoped to establish a 'think tank' to produce ideas for the 1990s. The latter suggestion brought a welter of questions about a possible conflict with the government. Childers frankly admitted his inability to speak the first official language. Mental pictures of an energetic first citizen, climbing, composing, conducting, digging a 'think tank', learning Irish and racing round the world promoting Ireland, ensured that humour was not lacking. An *Irish Times* photograph showing Mr Lynch looking heavenwards gave rise to suggestions that he was seeking divine backing for his colleague.

Criticism was soon forthcoming. Two nights later, addressing Kilbarrack Labour Party in his North East Dublin constituency, Dr Conor Cruise O'Brien, Minister for Posts and Telegraphs, suggested that Childers, if elected, might become the focus of a Fianna Fáil Government in exile. Cynically citing President Nixon's 'think tank' he spoke of neo-royalist concepts of the constitution. Foreign Affairs Minister Garret Fitzgerald echoed similar sentiments at Gort, Co. Galway, mentioning artificial and unreal conflict between government and president, and at Waterford the Taoiseach criticised previous Presidents as Fianna Fáil political pensioners.

The gleaming blue-and-gold luxury coach standing outside Leinster House in the middle of Saturday morning on 5 May immediately attracted attention. Labelled 'Erskine Childers, Presidential Election Coach' and equipped with table, easy chairs, telephone, television and expensive yellow carpeting, it smacked of hard salesmanship. Tricolours and loudspeakers projected from each side. Nobody apparently noticed any significance in the registration letters — 9999 RI!

Accompanied by Rita, Nessa and a granddaughter, Childers dutifully posed for photographs in the bus before being waved off by Maureen and Jack Lynch among a crowd of well-wishers. Immediate destination was Limerick, with calls *en route* at Clondalkin, Naas, Newbridge, Kildare, Portlaoise, Roscrea and Nenagh. As the vehicle threaded its way through the Dublin suburbs the reluctant candidate experienced a spasm of self-doubt. Looking earnestly at Rita he quietly said, 'You know I have made a grave mistake. Always I have fought on policies, now I am projecting myself. I have neither the charisma of Jack Lynch nor the mystique of Dev.' Doubts began to be dispelled after a successful day in Limerick and confidence grew as the entourage, reminiscent of an American Presidential cavalcade, moved on through Kerry into Cork. Fine Gael Deputy Michael Begley, Parliamentary Secretary to the Minister for Local Government, was quick to label the coach a 'wanderly wagon', the title of an RTE television children's puppet show.

Everywhere walkabouts in towns and villages were accompanied by the exhausting business of handshaking and autograph-signing. Short speeches usually painted a verbal picture of looking into the fire and seeing what lay in store for Irish children and grandchildren and seemed to strike a chord in young and old alike. Time was of the essence and the schedule had to be strictly adhered to. Thus it was arranged that Rita would gently pull her husband's jacket when the time allotted for his speech had expired and he was to stop. On one occasion an elderly spectator was heard to remark, 'Sure, why doesn't she let the poor man alone?'

The visit to Ennis, county town of Clare, on 8 May 1973 was a typical whistle-stop as the convoy made its way northwards from Limerick, having paused briefly at Shannon Airport, Newmarket-on-Fergus and Clarecastle. Just after 10.30 a.m. the brash-looking spectacle swung into O'Connell Square, traditional music by the *Chieftains* blaring through the loudspeakers of the coach. Childers stepped from one of the following cars and began to address the small gathering. His solemn, dignified manner and cultured English accent contrasted with almost everything else. In recalling his first visit to Ennis in August 1924, when de Valera had especially asked him to be present at the historic meeting after his release from

173

gaol, he was carefully stressing the link with Dev in the heart of the Chief's old constituency. After some remarks about Ireland in the 1990s, and a short walkabout, Erskine called at the Convent of Mercy to meet the nonagenarian Sister Aloysius before the convoy sped away towards Kilrush.

Photographs of Erskine Childers with Mother Mary and Mother Lelia of the Sacred Heart duly adorned the front page of the *Clare Champion*, which carried an in-depth interview with the candidate. He told the reporter of his envy of the orchestral conductor, which led on to the help he had given to the Radio Éireann singers.[4] Being able to associate himself with local projects proved a great asset wherever he went; in Clare the Shannon Industrial Estate and a new Old People's Home at Kilrush were natural talking-points. At the Waterford Crystal Factory it was gratifying to be told by Labour supporters that he would have their votes as the man who had removed discrimination from the health service.

Correspondence in the national press centred around the paradox that the party dedicated to restoration of Irish were fielding a candidate unable to utter even a few elementary phrases in the first official language. But few Republicans could in all conscience vote for O'Higgins. An odd 'Englishman' jibe crept in, and the *Munster Express* in a vitriolic attack referred to 'long-winded, well-worded speeches and Oxford modulated tones'.[5] Tremendous publicity ensued for O'Higgins at the televised Fine Gael Ard Fheis at Dublin Mansion House a few days before the presidential election. Some swipes were taken at President de Valera, and Minister for Finance, Richie Ryan, stirred up echoes of the past by declaring that O'Higgins came from Irish stock and would have been kept outside the pale when foreigners were in Ireland. After Fianna Fáil protests at the blatant electioneering Childers was allowed an additional half-hour television broadcast in which he reminded viewers that O'Higgins had declined to debate with him before the cameras.

174

Once the Ard Fheis euphoria abated there was a feeling that O'Higgins had, perhaps, peaked too early, and confidence grew in the Childers camp. The Government appeared to have erred in regarding the result as a vote of confidence, the *Irish Times* observing that the public might 'feel it is time they reasserted an element of principle by refusing to allow any party ever again to capture all the top posts'.[6] Expansion of the Presidential role tended to be played down during the last days of the campaign and Childers concentrated on social issues. At Sligo he expressed fears that young people were turning away from the Church, stressing that he was standing as a committed Christian:

The President, as the first citizen, and like all people imperfect in character, tinged with the deficiencies of human personality, must try to live up to the expectations of all those people who voted for him and for all the rest of the people. If elected, he must try and reflect in his personality all the most Christian attributes of the people as a whole. He must ensure that in a world of protest, stress and strain, those working for a more Christian civilisation are appreciated.[7]

In an interview in the *Catholic Standard* Childers said he would oppose 'certain secularist trends repugnant both to Catholics and Protestants'. On the North there was a commitment to use the office of President to try and build a bridge across partition and to assist in laying the foundations of a new Ireland built on a policy of national reconciliation. In many ways statements emanating from the two candidates were interchangeable, as three random quotations from O'Higgins's countrywide tour amply demonstrate; perhaps an increasingly worried O'Higgins was trying to steal some of his opponent's good ideas.

At Cavan:

I see Aras an Uachtaráin as an open house where Irishmen of varying beliefs and outlooks can meet and talk, with no strings, no pre-conditions.

At Arklow, Co. Wicklow:

An active President will be in touch with the young. We need to get the vitality and idealism of our young people working to make this island a better place.

At Youghal, Co. Cork:

The President can do a lot to further Ireland's interest abroad — to tell the story of our people, to remove misconceptions, to promote goodwill for the nation and its products.

But more and more such platitudes, however well meant, became irrelevant as the choice became one between personalities.

Childers's tour concluded with a rally at Cork on 28 May, where he also enjoyed himself hugely with students at University College, proving the equal of all comers and demonstrating the speed of his mental reactions. Jack Lynch exhorted the faithful and uncommitted, reminding them that Wolfe Tone could not speak Irish and Pádraig Pearse's father was English. Implicit admission that Erskine Childers senior was English appeared to vindicate Arthur Griffith after 51 years!

Official Fianna Fáil election literature seemed to pander to Irish susceptibilities and primitive anti-British feeling. Part of the information about the candidate's background was suspect (he did not 'live in County Wicklow from an early age'), part technically correct though misleading ('his mother was Irish'). After a life devoted unswervingly to Ireland and its interests, thirty-five years as a Dáil Deputy and twenty-two years in Government, it was still considered prudent to gloss over English birth, upbringing and education. Childers was periodically asked directly whether he was an Irishman, ancestry being for some voters a more important criterion on which to judge a Presidential candidate than a lifetime of toil and effort and the fact that every fibre in his body identified with Ireland. Such is the sad prejudice which lies just beneath the surface of Anglo-Irish relations.

Despite heavy rain about 2,000 people gathered in

College Green, Dublin for Fianna Fáil's final rally. Flanked on the platform by Lynch, Colley and Lenihan, all of whom spoke, Childers delivered a wide-ranging oration, quoting an essay by Thomas Davis from the volume given to him by Eamon de Valera. This was a subtle touch again, linking him with the retiring President and likely to strike a chord in the hearts of all Fianna Fáil faithful. By contrast the Coalition were under cover half a mile away at Liberty Hall, having first marched from Parnell Square led by Liam Cosgrave.

Voters in all thirty-two counties of Ireland headed for the polls on 30 May 1973, for in the North the newly styled local councils were also being elected. Erskine and Rita Childers voted early at the booth in Tranquila National School, Upper Rathmines Road, where they were greeted by local Deputy Ben Briscoe. Photographers pounced as the candidate chatted outside to a young lady from Achill. Turn-out in Dublin generally was low, which spelt a warning to the coalition.

As the first results trickled through early the following afternoon it became obvious that the favourite was in trouble. Constituency by constituency O'Higgins's vote was well down on 1966, with Dún Laoghaire–Rathdown and Cork City providing the biggest shocks. In his native city O'Higgins's vote dropped 7.3 per cent, and apart from Dublin he only headed the poll in South West Cork, Mayo, Roscommon–Leitrim and Wexford. At the end of the day, in a 61.9 per cent poll, Childers received 52 per cent of the votes cast, giving him a hefty 48,584 vote majority.

The victor, quietly confident for over a week, was nevertheless surprised by the margin. During the afternoon he slipped out of Fianna Fáil Mount Street Headquarters for a quiet cup of coffee with his wife and daughter, whose support and encouragement had never been greater. They were seated beside him at the subsequent news conference when he referred to 'the real sense of affectionate support'. Childers said he owed much to the wide contacts made as a Minister and the votes of women, who apparently liked

177

his voice. Never wanting for an apt analogy he confided to the press conference that he felt like a humble clerk who found himself in a palace after having a wand waved over him. Looking to the past he recalled that it was exactly fifty years to the day since the Civil War ended and then thanked O'Higgins for conducting the election at the very highest level of democratic debate. Mr Lynch seized the opportunity of pointing out that but for the vagaries of proportional representation Fianna Fáil would still be in power — a contention challenged by the Taoiseach, Liam Cosgrave. In evening television interviews on R.T.E. 'Involvement' and B.B.C. 'Midweek' there already seemed to be a 'father figure' image about the President-elect.

For Tom O'Higgins it was a bitter disappointment. He had fought a good campaign though generally below the 1966 standard. In an effort to win support from young people he was tempted to adopt a back-slapping approach which did not come naturally. His efforts reached a climax at the Ard Fheis where the misdirected enthusiasm of some colleagues led to indiscretions. Labour supporters at the grass roots were clearly unenthusiastic. Undoubtedly, too, he suffered from not having been in government for sixteen years. With no seat in the Twentieth Dáil, his political future looked bleak.

Undoubtedly Erskine's well-known public image had assisted him enormously. As Deputy Prime Minister he had enjoyed great publicity during the preceding four years, especially in the aftermath of the 1970 arms crisis, garnering a personal following in the process. Throughout he campaigned with a quiet dignity, concentrating on Ireland's future and his concern for religion, youth, recreation and peace. In some ways his campaign captured the imagination of the people and his mastery of the television medium must have played a part. Far from being a handicap the English accent proved an asset. He was able to influence people and at the end of the day they were not really interested in peripheral details such as ancestry and an ability to speak Irish. A President should

Erskine H. Childers
Fourth President of Ireland
A portrait by David Hone R.H.A.

be someone different and Childers clearly appealed in this respect.

There was a general welcome for the result, though the *Irish Independent* commented on the lack of interest shown by young people and thought that O'Higgins had peaked too soon. The Ard Fheis mud-slinging was roundly condemned and a cartoon depicted the President-elect poring over a book, saying to himself *'agam, agat, aige, aici . . .'*.[8] Though the electorate had chosen decisively a non-Irish speaker the *Irish Times,* perhaps churlishly, devoted a paragraph of its leader to the subject.[9] The *Irish Press* thought the electorate had proved again to be one of the most sophisticated in the world and had chosen the candidate with a wider range of government experience, achievement and greater urbanity than his opponent.[10] More was made of the fact that he was a Protestant by the press in Britain and America than at home. A Belgian radio commentator actually said it was as if the College of Cardinals, on the death of the Pope, were to elect a Freemason.

Erskine Childers was not in the Dáil on 5 June when Fianna Fáil colleagues applauded the official announcement of his victory. Many of those dutifully clapping had sat in stony silence on occasions in the recent past listening to him urge a peaceful approach to the North. Ironically a man whose dovelike view had often been derided was the one giving the party a tonic when it was most needed. After forty years' membership Erskine's last formal link with Fianna Fáil was broken a few days later when he resigned as a vice-president of the party and as the deputy for Monaghan.

After an arduous campaign involving some 350 speeches, endless travel, countless handshakes, numerous photographs, several television appearances and sundry other tensions, many men half Erskine's age would have felt utterly exhausted. But lifelong attention to physical fitness undoubtedly paid dividends, though a few days of peace and quiet after the heat of the battle were a necessity. Thus as Post Office vans delivered hundreds of letters of congratulations to 68 Highfield Road, the Childers family slipped quietly away to the one place they knew where it would be possible to stand apart for a few days and recoup resources, think, plan and relax — Glendalough House. By this time Robert Childers had retired from business in London and moved to Glendalough with his wife to enjoy a new role as a farmer, helping Robert Barton to administer the estate. Barton, in his ninety-third year frail but hearty, gained immense satisfaction from his cousin's success. As best man and closest lifelong friend of the elder Erskine he had lived on to see Ireland make amends as best it could for the dreadful happenings of half a century before.

The first three weeks of June passed quickly. Among many practical problems, such as selling the house and arranging the removal of furniture and effects, no small task after forty years in the same residence, there was something else niggling at Erskine. The Constitution provided for the Presidential Declaration of Office to be given in Irish or English but as the three previous incumbents had chosen the first official language he could do no other. Time had to be given to perfecting his pronunciation which, like many Anglo-Saxons, he found difficult to master and a tape recording was obtained from a native speaker in West Cork. The President-elect and his wife spent several quiet days staying near Sneem on the Kerry coast, and Erskine's first halting attempts were made on the rocky shore where the only distraction was the sound of waves breaking.

Since colonial trappings vanished Dublin has been short of pageantry, even of the sort of ceremonial pomp and circumstance seen daily in London and other capital cities. Inauguration of a new President brings a brief touch of colour to the grey city, an essentially Irish occasion making few headlines elsewhere, though the fourth President, Erskine Hamilton Childers, was pleased to receive messages from world leaders including Queen Elizabeth, President Nixon (then under investigation by a Senate Committee for his role in Watergate), President Podgorny of Russia, President Pompidou of France, General Franco of Spain and President Bhutto of Pakistan. The spectacle commenced in mid-morning when Erskine and Rita Childers emerged from their suburban house for the last time, pausing to wave to the crowd of some 200 neighbours and wellwishers before entering the dark blue Presidential vintage Rolls Royce.

If Erskine Childers embodied a fusion of cultures, St Patrick's Cathedral, Dublin on the morning of Monday, 25 June 1973 encompassed similar variety when the congregation for an Inter-Denominational Service gathered prior to the Presidential inauguration. This reflected a growth of ecumenism and tolerance in Church affairs since Dr Hyde's inauguration thirty-five years before, which by coincidence, had been the first formal occasion attended by Childers as a public representative, just eight days after his election as a Dáil Deputy. Then, the Taoiseach, Eamon de Valera, and members of the Government had attended a Solemn Votive Mass in the Pro-Cathedral rather than take part in a Service at St Patrick's.

Now, in 1973, President de Valera and members of the Government were seated beneath the banners of the Knights of St Patrick, the Royal Standards and the tattered Union flags of the defunct Southern Irish Regiments. Cardinal Conway, Archbishop of Armagh and Primate of All Ireland, together with Archbishop Ryan of Dublin and the Apostolic Nuncio, represented the Roman Catholic Church. President-elect and Mrs Childers were the last to arrive, greeted at the door by Dean Griffin and escorted to the erstwhile Royal pew. The Introit, 'O Jerusalem, Jerusalem is built as a city that is at unity in itself', set the theme of the Service, Childers himself having selected the devotional readings. He personally read a number of prayers, one found by Lady Wilde in the west of Ireland, one recorded by Dr Hyde and Lady Gregory's version of St Patrick's Breastplate, whilst dignitaries of the Methodist, Lutheran and Presbyterian Churches, the Salvation Army and the Society of Friends all took part. To Erskine's bitter disappointment the three Roman Catholic prelates declined to play an active part in the service.

The subsequent brief inauguration ceremony took place in St Patrick's Hall at Dublin Castle, for centuries the seat and symbol of British rule, in the presence of the twelve persons required by the Constitution and other leading state figures. After Taoiseach Liam Cosgrave announced that Erskine Childers had been elected, the Chief Justice asked the President of the High Court to read the Declaration of Office to the President-elect, who repeated it in carefully rehearsed, impeccable Irish and then signed the Declaration. The Chief Justice presented the Seal of Office and after Cosgrave had spoken Erskine Childers replied:

Taoiseach, I am most grateful for your kind remarks. On behalf of my wife and myself, I thank you from my heart for your good wishes. I am greatly honoured at the attendance here today of so many distinguished personages. I appreciate your presence and am sincerely grateful to you all.

This has been for me a most moving ceremony, particularly in that June 25th is my father's birthday anniversary. I am humbly aware of the great honour conferred upon me at this ceremony. I know I shall need the prayers of the people for God's guidance in the performance of my duties and in making a meaningful contribution to the harmony among Irishmen and Irishwomen which we all desire. I do hope that you will all remember me in your prayers.

Eamon de Valera was my political mentor and leader and my friend for many years. I can testify to his statesmanlike counsel and above all to his kindness of heart. All of you here present have witnessed the dignity with which he graced the office of President during the past 14 years. I join with the Taoiseach in wishing Mr de Valera and his gracious wife every happiness in retirement.

A triumphant drive to the Presidential residence took the First Citizen and First Lady through Dublin streets thronged with applauding and cheering crowds, the scenes being replayed to the country at large for the first time by television. In Phoenix Park a 21-gun salute was fired by a detachment of Field Artillery. Once at Áras an Uachtaráin President Childers greeted his predecessor, Eamon de Valera, who was spending his first hour as a private citizen since he was elected Member of Parliament for East Clare in 1917. Afterwards he received members of the Council of State, the Government and his own family, regretting only that neither of his sons was able to be present. There followed a luncheon and the ceremonies concluded with a Government reception at Dublin Castle in the evening.

Throughout the day a spirit of ecumenism and conciliation had pervaded the ceremonies, only the Northern Unionists and extreme Republicans being absent. It was surely an occasion of which Erskine senior and Molly would have thoroughly approved, a poignant touch being the presence of Mr Cosgrave as Head of the Government of the day. There was certainly a fairy-tale aspect. Erskine's long journey which began as a bereaved English schoolboy in Norfolk had reached its climax and he was now Head of the State to which he had then improbably given his allegiance which never subsequently wavered. How perceptive had been Molly Childers in 1930 when she envisaged him as a teacher, a prophet and trainer outside the political arena (see page 69), inspiring youth by lectures and motivating people.

Chapter XII
A PRESIDENT FOR ALL THE NATION

As conceived under the 1937 Irish Constitution the Presidency is largely intended to represent the State in international courtesies. The President appoints the Taoiseach upon the advice of the Dáil, and Ministers on the advice of the Taoiseach, but his influence is essentially designed to be social rather than political. The Constitution provides in writing for functions which are exercised in a constitutional monarchy by the reigning sovereign, but the role and style of Ireland's Presidents have in practice been controversial, and they have sometimes appeared almost irrelevant to the nation, with its proud tradition of High Kings.

The President is allotted some powers but few of an absolute kind save the right to refer bills to the Supreme Court to determine their constitutionality, and the right to resign, both of which were exercised by President O'Dálaigh in 1976. It is probable that as he drafted the relevant Article 12, Eamon de Valera was conscious of his embarrassing wrangle with Governor-General James McNeill shortly after he took office in 1932. This had revolved around the refusal of Fianna Fáil Ministers to re-cognise the office of Governor-General and ended with McNeill challenging the authority of the Government. Clearly any possibility of a future clash between Government and Head of State was to be avoided and the latter was granted only very limited political powers.

All the President's other formal powers are exercised on the advice of the Government and he has no independent

executive powers other than discretion to refuse to dissolve
the Dáil and proclaim a general election when advised to
by a Taoiseach who has failed to retain the support of a
majority in the Dáil. This obliges the Taoiseach to resign,
giving the Dáil an opportunity to nominate a new Taoiseach for appointment by the President. Three discretionary
powers have only limited political significance.

Article 22 — Power to refer to a Committee of Privileges
appointed by him for that purpose, an appeal from the Seanad
against a certificate by the Chairman of the Dáil that a Bill is a
money Bill, a certificate which drastically curtails the legislative
power of the Seanad in respect of that Bill.
Article 24 — A President has power to decide whether time available to the Seanad for consideration of a Bill should be abridged
to an extent embodied in a resolution passed by the Dáil.
Article 27 — Power to withhold signature to a Bill if, on representation from a prescribed number of members of both Houses, he
is satisfied the Bill contains a proposal of such national importance that the will of the people thereon ought to be ascertained.

All three of the Presidents who spanned the first thirty-
five years' existence of the office maintained an un-
obtrusive approach, though they differed in background.
The first President, Dr Douglas Hyde, had tried to avoid
both party politics and controversy in a life devoted to
preserving Ireland's cultural heritage. A Protestant with
social roots in the *ancien régime,* he was a prudent and
popular agreed choice to inaugurate the Presidency.
Largely unknown outside the country, he was elderly and
inactive but his quiet dignity was reassuring throughout
the testing war years. After serving a seven-year term he
did not seek re-election in 1945.

Seán T. O'Kelly had been active in politics all his life,
loyal to Sinn Féin and Fianna Fáil. His candidacy in 1945
was hotly opposed by Fine Gael and the hard Republican
wing and his votes were in an over-all minority at the first
count. However, he proved as acceptable to the Inter-Party
Governments as to Fianna Fáil and was not opposed in

1952 when he sought a second seven-year term. During a visit to America in 1959 when he addressed a joint session of the United States Congress, President O'Kelly successfully persuaded Irish-Americans to stop financial aid to the I.R.A. at the time of the Border campaign, which won him much praise. But few would deny that this was a blatantly political act.

As principal architect of the Presidency Eamon de Valera must, presumably, be viewed as the ideal incumbent. Aged seventy-six at the start of his first seven-year term, he was already a legend and the most famous Irishman of his time. Despite advanced years and virtual blindness he undertook the endless round of social duties and, in the words of his official biographers, filled his office of President with dignity and charm.[1] This was reflected in the high standing of the Presidency when he retired in 1973.

On two occasions Presidential power to refer Bills to the Supreme Court had been invoked before 1973, each time by Dr Hyde and after consultation with the Council of State which first met on 8 January 1940.[2] An Offences Against the State Bill was then deemed to be Constitutional but some provisions of a School Attendance Bill, referred in February 1943, were found to be repugnant and did not pass into law. President de Valera twice consulted the Council of State, in June 1961 and March 1967, and on the latter occasion, though not referred to the Supreme Court, some offending sections of an Income Tax Bill were amended subsequently. The watchdog function was seen to be impartial and afforded necessary protection to the populace.

An objective view of the Presidency, given in a Thomas Davis lecture by Professor Desmond Williams broadcast during the 1973 election campaign, adjudged it to be relatively weak compared with the headship of other states and its practical significance in Irish affairs to be unaltered by the passage of time.[3] It was scrutinised during Tom O'Higgins's campaign in 1966 when his relative youth and vigour and advocacy of an expanded Presidency contrasted sharply with the elderly Mr de Valera and appealed to younger people especially.

Erskine Childers's first public comment on the Presidency was reported during the June 1945 election campaign when Seán T. O'Kelly successfully stood against Seán MacEoin of Fine Gael and Dr Patrick MacCartan. Speaking at Ballinalee he defined the three functions of the Head of State:

The first function is common to all democratic heads of States whether King or President. He was elected by the people as a symbol of all that was best in an Irishman and he became the Chief Citizen of the land. Once President he became the symbol of the people and whenever his name was mentioned and wherever he appeared his presence should divert men from thinking of themselves and cause them to consider their duties as citizens and their position as Irishmen. The second function of the President was to act as the protector of the people against possible wrong-doing by the Seanad or the Dáil. The third function was that of being the nation's chief host to foreign guests and while giving royal hospitality to tell such people in their own language of Ireland's aspirations, her problems and her attitude towards the world outside. [4]

Twenty-eight years later Mr. Childers genuinely believed that the Presidency might be developed to play a more positive role in the life of the Nation, a role which appealed enormously to him. He envisaged the holder of the office as a leader outside politics and a focal point of cultural and environmental issues, reflecting the aspirations of the people on matters where discussion and debate would not create division but encourage enlightened examination. Like O'Higgins he saw no reason why the Presidential residence could not be a meeting-place where people of differing views, say on the North, could talk together. It was, he believed, all a question of how broadly the constitutional limitations were interpreted.

As the Presidency was taken off the shelf, dusted down and subjected to detailed examination, Erskine's concept of a broader role became more ambitious. His 'think-tank' suggestion attracted criticism from members of the Coalition Government as likely to lead to Constitutional conflict, but as O'Higgins's campaign was based on a similar expansionist theme in both 1966 and 1973 this was necessarily muted. At the end of the day if he won, his wings could be clipped within hours of taking office by a few casual twists of the Constitutional vice and innovative enthusiasm effectively stifled.

If the Irish Constitution ensures that the Presidency is limited in a political sense, successive Governments have ensured that its style and circumstances have been likewise restricted. Lavish expenditure disappeared with the Vice-Royalty and the material trappings of the Presidential household are minimal. Indeed, compared with the expenditure of many nations on a Head of State, Ireland looks positively parsimonious. Even within the constraints of an Irish budget the amount is relatively small, being in 1973 only marginally more than a quarter of the sum allotted to run the Dublin National Gallery. In addition to the President's salary and expenses it has to cover the cost of all domestic requirements, including the wages of household staff and the chauffeur.

The vast ninety-four-roomed mansion, largely dating from the mid-eighteenth century and standing in isolated splendour within Dublin's Phoenix Park, was for long the residence of successive British Viceroys and is still commonly referred to as 'the Lodge'. After the resignation of the second Governor-General, James McNeill, in 1932, it stood empty for six years until, renamed Áras an Uachtaráin, it became the official Presidential residence. Upkeep and maintenance of the fabric and expensive security arrangements dissipate money which might be expended on other aspects of the Presidency. The establishment is modest and when Erskine Childers took office administration was in the hands of just six civil servants, comprising the President's Secretary, an assistant secretary, personal secretary, typist, switchboard operator and a messenger. Press and public relations advisers and speechwriters, considered an indispensable part of the retinue of national leaders almost everywhere else in the western world, were unheard of. The eight domestic staff who lived in enjoyed no pension rights or retirement provisions and with long, irregular hours needed to be utterly dedicated people. Two military *aides-de-camp* were seconded from the Army and twenty-four-hour security was the responsibility of the Garda Síochána (police).

Like all new incumbents the Childers family struggled to familiarise themselves as rapidly as possible with the geography of the house, the staff and the rigid protocol that everyday life demanded. Their own quarters comprised a comfortable upstairs apartment in the west wing and a separate flat for Nessa. A story of historical interest was connected with almost every room, and Erskine was soon a mine of information about the vice-regal past. A typical day began at about 7.30 with prayers, the Presidential Chaplain being Canon E. M. Neill, Rector of St Brigid's Church, Castleknock where the President worshipped when in residence and read the lesson most Sundays.

After breakfast the morning was usually devoted to office duties, dealing with correspondence, examining and signing Bills sent from the Oireachtas, studying Dáil and Seanad Reports and reading the daily newspapers. In the early days a large number of private congratulatory greetings from far and near were systematically acknowledged, and a regular volume of correspondence was received from members of the public who were aggrieved by some official action or inaction. Such mail could only be forwarded on to the Government for attention as a President has no power to intervene. Periodically a newly-accredited Ambassador called to present his credentials, and the whole Diplomatic Corps was received each New Year.

Afternoons were reserved for outside duties or receiving visitors and the early evening was frequently the only opportunity to snatch a few private minutes of relaxation. Informal dinner-parties for up to sixteen guests took place about four times a month, the President himself enjoying much discretion in the issue of invitations, although he was expected to entertain new Ambassadors soon after their arrival in Dublin. In a country which does not legally recognise divorce the situation for a divorcee can sometimes be difficult. But President Childers never felt inhibited by the marital status of a prospective guest, and one divorced lady was amazed to receive a summons to dine at Áras an Uachtaráin, at first presuming it to be a practical joke perpetrated by her ex-husband!

An almost complete loss of privacy and freedom of action represented the greatest contrast to the life that Erskine Childers had known hitherto. He was used to an amount of daily travel, commuting between home and office, office and the Dáil, free within a broad framework to plan his own day and initiate engagements and appointments. Henceforth he could only wait for invitations to arrive and then accept or decline on the advice of his Secretary. Mealtimes were no longer elastic. Official communication with the Government was through the Taoiseach's Office and speeches had to be vetted and approved before delivery. Practice dictated that about once a month the Taoiseach called to apprise the President of domestic and foreign affairs, a custom initiated by Mr de Valera during Dr Hyde's period of office. But such briefings from Liam Cosgrave, containing little more than could be gleaned from the newspapers, were small compensation to a man who had thrived on making and implementing policy and motivating a major department of state.

The first few weeks of Childers's Presidency established the pattern which characterised his short term of office. An energetic approach and high-minded determination to play a more meaningful part in the life of the Nation by taking the Presidency to the people lay behind every action and for some time the ambition lingered of becoming a true leader outside and above domestic politics. Three days after inauguration Princess Grace of Monaco became the first official overseas visitor to be received by the new President and First Lady, followed twenty-four hours later by a visit to Galway for the first official outside duty.

Opening the Leisureland recreation and entertainment complex on the sea-front at Salthill fulfilled an election promise though at the cost of some embarrassment to the Government. After Erskine had pledged himself to open Leisureland if he became President, it was learned that Signor F. X. Ortoli, President of the E.E.C. Commission, was planning to make his first official visit to Ireland on the same day. Such an important visitor would expect to be received by the Head of State but Childers remained adamant that he was committed to go to Galway and the crisis was only resolved when Sr Ortoli postponed his visit because of a (diplomatic) illness.

But if Erskine had his way over Leisureland the Government proved less sympathetic a few weeks later. During a recorded interview for American radio on the subject of Northern Ireland he suggested that the violence had postponed reunification. There had to be collaboration and co-operation in the North before any prospect of reunification, and British troops could not be withdrawn and should not be withdrawn from Northern Ireland because if they were withdrawn there might be sectarian violence of an extreme character.

Such a view found broad agreement among politicians and public alike and could not be interpreted as controversial by any stretch of the imagination. Throughout the interview the President stressed that he was not giving his own opinion but acting as a rapporteur of the Irish situation as he saw it and confining his answers to matters about which all parties were united in policy. The offer to act as a mediator and use his residence for meetings merely repeated election pledges, while an appeal to Americans not to subscribe to relief projects as the money might be utilised to purchase arms echoed President O'Kelly's call of fourteen years before. Yet it brought a sharp reminder that all scripts should be submitted for vetting by the Government and no more radio interviews about the Northern situation must be given. The Constitutional vice was tightened half a notch by a Government that had little interest in the Presidency or the ideas of the new incumbent.

If Erskine's erstwhile vision of a super-peacemaker President quickly faded, modest efforts towards a positive contribution to the Northern problem continued. Belfast Rotary Club, the Divis Street Players and Belfast Trade Unionists featured among groups formally received and welcomed to Áras an Uachtaráin. The most prominent individual Northern visitor was Lord O'Neill of the Maine, who called in August 1973 and again about a year later. The former Stormont Prime Minister had been one of the first people to publicly tip Erskine Childers for the Presidency in some jocular asides at a Publicity Club of Ireland luncheon in Dublin in January 1971. Later that year Lord O'Neill had made an unpublicised call on President de Valera, so he was already familiar with the large house.

During a wide-ranging discussion President Childers and Lord O'Neill touched on many subjects, but the latter recalls that his pessimism about Northern Ireland seemed to surprise his host. Áras an Uachtaráin provided a link between them as Lord O'Neill recalled that his maternal grandfather, the Earl of Crewe, had lived there as Viceroy from 1892 to 1895 and his mother spent some of her childhood years at 'the Lodge'. Erskine responded by musing that his own kinsman, the statesman Hugh Childers, was Chairman of the Committee on Financial Relations during the same period and must have visited 'the Lodge' when in Dublin. On his second visit Lord O'Neill observed, while strolling in the grounds, that plaques commemorating the planting of trees by members of the Royal family had been cleaned up after years of neglect so that even the Anglo-Irish tradition flickered fitfully as Erskine Childers genuinely tried to be a President for all the Nation. But any hope of an impact on the North was negligible as Unionist intransigence destroyed the slender framework of the Sunningdale Agreement. A vivid reminder of the recurring violence came with a visit to Monaghan on a chill winter morning for the funeral of the murdered Senator Billy Fox, when Erskine joined politicians from both sides of the Border in the tiny Church at Aughnamullen near Ballybay.

By October 1973 when, for once, no press photographers were in attendance at the Abbey Theatre for a Presidential visit to see *The Importance of Being Earnest*, Erskine was in danger of overexposure. Unprecedented activity by the First Citizen and First Lady, including a large number of engagements outside Dublin, had the media scrambling for fresh angles. Among many and varied activities he had been pictured forest-walking in County Wicklow, fishing off Killybegs in Co. Donegal, planting a tree outside a Trades Union office in Dublin, admiring a cauliflower at Lough Egish Co-operative, Co. Monaghan, and canoeing on the Vartry Reservoir, in addition to more routine plaque-unveilings and formal visits. The heavy tide of engagements ran on and on: opening a museum at Tuam, Co. Galway; attending the finals of the National Public Speaking Competition at Thurles, Co. Tipperary; at Mass prior to the start of restoration work at Duiske Abbey, Co. Kilkenny; addressing a reunion of past pupils at the Salesian College in Pallaskenry, Co. Limerick, and attending centenary celebrations at St Patrick's College, Cavan — were all part of a President's work in 1973–74.

Third-world politics intruded peripherally. A State reception was held at Shannon Airport for General Gowon of Nigeria who was en route to Ottawa for the Commonwealth Prime Ministers' Conference. But the World Ploughing Championships at Wellingtonbridge, Co. Wexford were not graced by the Presidential presence owing to the fact that an all-white team from Rhodesia was competing.

The arts, especially music and poetry, were encouraged in every way possible. At the Ninth Grand Canal Fiesta at Robertstown, Co. Kildare, a large crowd witnessed the unusual spectacle of a Head of State reading poetry, moreover works that he had selected himself, including items by Thomas Kinsella, Francis Ledwidge, James Stephens, Pádraig Pearse and W. B. Yeats and translations by his predecessor Dr Hyde. Visits to Christ Church Cathedral, Dublin were always welcome and an opportunity to see an old friend, Dean Salmon, whom Erskine first knew as Rector of St. Ann's Church in Dawson Street where he had worshipped regularly. Giving the Christmastide lecture there in 1973 provided another chance to read publicly from his grandmother's anthology.

In the manner of cultured European heads of state President Childers introduced a new dimension to Dublin life by inviting performers to Áras an Uachtaráin. The Great Reception Room echoed to the strains of Haydn, Mozart, Honegger and a little-known work by an Irish composer, Arthur Duff, when the New Irish Chamber Orchestra gave a concert there in July 1974 before an invited audience on the eve of its departure to play in the Paris Summer Festival. Not only top-ranking musicians benefited. The Greenfield Boys Choir from northside Dublin, all treble voices and painstakingly trained by a dedicated amateur in his spare time, were invited to sing, giving a couple of dozen youngsters an event to remember all their lives. A tremendous boost was given to the morale of Irish artists whatever their standing. The publicity and patronage were important and in a broader sense the Presidency itself was enhanced. Active Presidential support was given to events such as the Killarney Bach Festival and the Wexford Festival of Grand Opera.

By the end of his first year in office President Childers had attended 210 functions and visited sixty-five community or social councils in addition to eighty-seven other organisations in all parts of the country. Over 4,500 visitors had been received. Such impressive statistics reflected dedication and sheer hard work. Yet, it was obvious that any serious idea of expanding the Presidency to be an effective force on national issues was stillborn, at least until the return of a Fianna Fáil Government, and unusual and potentially invaluable personal links with different Irish traditions could not be capitalised upon. Constrictions seemed endless, all invitations were closely vetted and the Presidential Secretariat had a far stronger hand than that of a State Department. Even a simple request such as provision of a porter to assist visitors and undertake various heavy duties at Áras an Uachtaráin led to endless, frustrating correspondence with the Government.

But it was alien to Erskine's nature to sit back and allow his Presidency to assume the stultifying tranquillity associated with his predecessors. Though more or less limited to influencing environmental or social issues Erskine never betrayed any hint of pent-up frustration. Constructive thought on issues such as community welfare, use of leisure time and retention of an environmental 'Irishness' could in some measure shape the future, and dedication and idealism were transmitted to audiences everywhere as the self-imposed schedule of engagements continued. Opening a community hall in memory of the 1916 Patriot, Con Colbert, at Athea, Co. Limerick in January 1974, Childers pledged to spend the rest of his term of office in encouraging voluntary organisations to play as much a part as any other authority in developing the character of the younger generation and caring for old people and those in difficulty.[5]

There were private moments, as with most men approaching their seventieth year, when Erskine would look back and reflect on his unusual life. Memories were stirred, as when the twelve-year-old daughter of the family living in his parents' former house in Bushy Park Road came to present old letters and papers relating to the Anglo-Irish War which had been discovered under floorboards. A visit by members of the Ancient and Honorable Artillery

Company of Massachusetts provided another poignant reminder of his parents' chance meeting some 70 years before. Strolling in the grounds one day he asked his wife if she believed his parents knew of his success for he still found difficulty in accepting his own exalted position.

Controversial aspects of Ireland's past were always played down, even if his parents were involved. An Australian journalist who had known them in 1921 anticipated talking about those troubled times when he took tea at Áras an Uachtaráin. Instead the President spoke mainly about his Yorkshire ancestors and the stallion 'Flying Childers' with a reputed 600,000 pedigreed descendants on the racecourses of the world.[6] Another visitor momentarily embarrassed his host when he found a faded inscription on the back of an old photograph of Erskine senior. Magnus Magnusson, of B.B.C. television 'Mastermind' fame, was preparing an article on father and son for the *Radio Times* to coincide with a reading of *The Riddle of the Sands* on Radio 4 when he found words with a decidedly anti-British slant, written by someone in the emotion of the Civil War. At first Childers was adamant that it should not be alluded to under any circumstances but he relented after Magnusson pointed out that it symbolised for him how the President had helped to bury the passions of the past.[7]

Contemporary and future aspects of life in Ireland were greater preoccupations, and President Childers had a positive message wherever he went. With the advent of technology indicating an increase in leisure time he was concerned with its constructive use and often spoke of his surprise that new housing estates were built without the provision of adequate recreational facilities.

Those who go to work for a living have 161 days of leisure out of a total 365 days and the character of our society depends so much on what we do with our spare time. People have not really thought about this. I see myself as a catalyst, a generative force encouraging people to use their leisure time to the best advantage. Undoubtedly it will be costly but young people must be encouraged in this vital area on a scale which we can afford. I have noticed that few people seem to realise that no government can create the character of society. The character of human society and the kind of world we're going to have in 1990 is decided by people — by individual conduct and the action of every single person ... It is up to the older group in the community working with the younger people, to ensure that we avoid the horrors that can be seen abroad by preserving a Christian society on the basis of a community working together. [8]

Visits to Cork to inaugurate a youth project and to Galway opening the first stage of an extension to University College in autumn 1974 provided platforms to call for an in-depth study of the sociological attitudes of the young to determine whether educational methods prepared them to face the world of the 1990s. Irish thought and action needed to be stimulated. Childers believed that working in smaller communities engendered a feeling of belonging and offered the best chance of escaping or counteracting contemporary 'rat race' pressures. Learning how to relax and unwind, temperance, selectivity in reading and cultivating a love of music were other remedies advocated.

At a conference of the International Association for the Study of Anglo-Irish Literature in Cork Childers sparked off a discussion by asking if pop songs had any significance and might be linked with myth. The pop cult and its appeal and influence was of genuine interest and no mere 'sop' to appear up-to-date. A visiting priest was surprised to find himself being quizzed by the President about the origins of songs and names of singers, as His Excellency made copious notes to augment the rudimentary knowledge acquired from Nessa or his grandchildren. Erskine Childers never fell into the trap of patronising children and young people either to their faces or when talking about their needs. Soon after a television appearance in which he indicated that young people were welcome at the Presidential residence, however, his sincerity was put to the test. One Sunday four boys knocked on the West Wing door and said that they had come to visit the President.

Unfortunately Mr Childers was away for the week-end but the youngsters were invited inside and given some light refreshments, a casual enquiry revealing that they were up from the country for the Scientist of the Year competition and had 'climbed the gate'. For good measure they added that 'the President invited us on the telly'.

No invitation was too humble or insignificant to be ignored. When he travelled to Rathdrum, Co. Wicklow in August 1973 to open the First Parnell Youth Games of the local Youth Club, President Childers could not have imagined the lasting impact of his interest and support. Yet each year since his death the boys and girls have marked the anniversary by a wreath-laying ceremony, such was their appreciation of the man and his ideals. Lecturing on 'Our Architectural Heritage' at the Royal Dublin Society he told an audience of youngsters that his first action if he was Dictator of Ireland would be to ban the use of dull, muddy, grey, depressing paint on houses and cottages and order that they be painted in bright colours.[9] Students visiting Áras an Uachtaráin and expecting to shock with their 'revolutionary' views sometimes departed amazed by the President's knowledge of revolution and cogent argument for moderation.

Friends and family sometimes wondered about the gruelling schedule that Erskine set himself and there can be no doubt he felt pressures, even questioning whether his reactions and responses were sufficiently Presidential. Opportunities for 'escape' were limited. There is no rural retreat to which to repair within Ireland and Government permission is required to leave the country. Officialdom and detectives were always on hand. Only in the apartment or the grounds was a measure of privacy afforded, but in August 1974 a few quiet days were spent in Castlegregory on the Dingle Peninsula in County Kerry. Relatively free from constraints the President amazed other visitors by his energy, rising at the crack of dawn to walk miles before breakfast with security men panting to keep up the pace. From Kerry the Presidential party moved north to Donegal, where the artist Derek Hill hosted a short stay at his cottage in Churchill. A helicopter took them on to Tory Island for a tour by tractor and trailer, pausing for Mr Hill to make preliminary sketches for his portrait of Erskine which subsequently hung at Áras an Uachtaráin for some years.

Two overseas visits were surrounded by protocol and formality. The funeral of President Pompidou in Paris in April 1974 meant a fleeting reunion with the French capital which held so many memories. A lonely travel agent who some forty years before had wandered through the Bois de Boulogne with holes in his socks was now received like visiting Royalty, yet the dream was a reality and there could be no quick look at old haunts, though there was time for a chat with Dr Hillery, attending in his capacity as Vice-president of the European Commission.

As if to emphasise that Ireland had arrived in Europe it fell appropriately to Erskine Childers to become the first State Visitor to another European country when, together with his wife and a small Irish contingent, he left Dublin for Brussels for a four-day stay in May 1974. All the pomp and splendour essential to such occasions surrounded President and Mrs Childers, who stayed at the Laeken Palace. Personal relationships with King Baudouin and Queen Fabiola were particularly warm. Visits to Hainaut and Tournai, a night at the Opera and a performance of 'Here are the Ladies' by Siobhán McKenna at the Palace were interspersed with banquets and receptions and a further meeting with Dr Hillery, who was accompanied by other Irish members of the E.E.C. Commission. The President was honoured to receive the Grand Cordon of the Order of Leopold. The *Irish Times* summed up the visit:

It was the first airing of an Irish President in Europe and Mr Childers acquitted himself well, moving from reanimation of the perpetual flame to signatures on golden books, the exchanges of gifts and civilities with royal and civic dignitaries and reviews of troops as if such activities were part of the normal drill of an old Fianna Fáil warrior. [10]

During the flight across Britain a message of greeting was despatched to Queen Elizabeth and Erskine must have mused on the prospect of a stay at Buckingham Palace. Might there, by some remote possibility, be a sudden end to the centuries-long conflict between the land of his birth and the land that he had adopted and which, more significantly, had adopted him? The year had promised so much in the wake of the Sunningdale Agreement and yet as he glanced down at the newspapers by his side with headlines about the Ulster Workers Council strike threat the ominous implications were all too apparent. But though ceremonial London remained a misty vision a meeting with an influential member of the Royal family did take place on Irish soil.

Ireland's staunchest friend and unofficial ambassador at the Court of St. James was Earl Mountbatten of Burma. The Earl's wise counsel was sought on many matters and as a cousin of the Queen, uncle of the Duke of Edinburgh and mentor to Prince Charles he was one of the most influential Englishmen of his time. Through his late wife Edwina, daughter of a Tory M.P. and granddaughter of the German-born financier Sir Ernest Cassel, the Earl had inherited Broadlands Estate in Hampshire and Classiebawn Castle, near Cliffoney on the Sligo coast. Regular summer visits to the Castle, which stands high above the shore of Donegal Bay, continued despite the resurgence of trouble in the North and he scorned warnings about his vulnerability.

As well as spending much of his time sailing and fishing from near-by Mullaghmore Harbour, Earl Mountbatten took an interest in local events and was popular with his neighbours, many of whom he knew personally. The opening of a School of Landscape Painting exhibition at Summerhill College, Sligo seems an unlikely setting for a first meeting between an Irish President and British Royalty. Yet the cultures of the two nations are inseparably intertwined and it was here on 27 August 1974 that Erskine and Rita Childers greeted Earl Mountbatten and chatted cordially with him for some time.

The spacious grounds of Áras an Uachtaráin provided an ample challenge to a President who found relaxation and satisfaction in strenuous gardening. Stories of one potentially disastrous episode concerning Erskine Childers leaked out and, suitably embellished, caused a few wry smiles in the corridors of Leinster House. As he stood in a small boat on the lake, lopping trees and bushes, a branch suddenly snapped sending him headlong into the water, to emerge covered in green slime. Rather than risk soiling the priceless Donegal carpets in the house and with as much Presidential dignity as he could muster in the circumstances Erskine removed most of his clothing before going indoors. Meanwhile security guards had been alerted that a figure in his underpants was prowling in the grounds and the resulting confrontation can best be left to the imagination!

A project which caught Erskine's imagination and one to which many patient hours were devoted was a swamp garden; and about the middle of November 1974 it was learned that some special plants for this would be arriving from England within a week. The news caused a flurry of activity, with the President devoting every possible daylight hour to energetic preparation despite an especially full diary. Wednesday (13 November) brought a party of officials from the Royal Dublin Society, ladies from the Ballivor Guild of the Irish Countrywomen's Association and the Brookville Ladies Club together with a visit from Bernard McDonagh, the Sligo artist, followed on Thursday (14 November) by ladies from the Navan and Croom Guilds of the I.C.A. In addition to the garden much time was being given to preparation of a speech to be delivered to the first Annual Dinner of the Irish Division of the Royal College of Psychiatrists the following Saturday, an event to which the President attached great importance.

Friday (15 November) was dominated by a luncheon visit by the French Prime Minister M. Jacques Chirac, together with a party of thirty-two people, and Erskine enjoyed a rare opportunity to speak French. During the lunch an official invitation was issued to the Childerses to visit France and there was some talk of a few private days being spent in the French countryside, though such an arrangement would have required Goverment approval. A dinner engagement with the Malahide Junior Chamber of Commerce proved rather more protracted than anticipated, and during her husband's speech Rita noticed that his breathing seemed hurried and his voice sounded thicker than usual.

Back home Erskine worked until almost 5 a.m. on his speech for the next evening dealing with the debilitating effects on national life of stress and job boredom. With a captive audience of psychiatrists it was a rare opportunity to hammer home points about which he had felt especially deeply since being Minister for Health. After some three hours' fitful sleep and a light breakfast he was out digging the swamp garden soon after dawn and with no official visitors the day was devoted to the project. It was mild and dry and two changes of clothing were required, each trip to the house producing cautionary strictures about 'overdoing it' and the ritual response of 'nonsense'.

With a developing interest in psychiatry, eighteen-year-old Nessa accompanied her father to the Psychiatrists' dinner held at the Royal College of Physicians in Kildare Street, just a stone's throw from Leinster House. Erskine Childers spoke passionately for twenty minutes to a warm and sympathetic audience, urging more research into the practice of relaxology, meditation and self-becalming to cope with the strains of modern life. He deplored the reliance placed on tranquillising drugs to alleviate anxiety and fear, and advocated planning for the more effective use of leisure time. Nobody present could fail to be aware of the intensity of the speaker's feelings but none was prepared for his immediate collapse as he sat down to enthusiastic applause.

At a medical gathering in a medical college both expert opinion and equipment were on hand and everything possible was done within minutes to assist the President.

During an ambulance dash to the Mater Hospital electric shocks were administered but failed to restore his heartbeat and all further efforts proved abortive. Just after 1 a.m. on the morning of Sunday, 17 November 1974, to the grief of a stunned family and an unprepared nation, a brief announcement confirmed that Erskine Hamilton Childers, President of Ireland, was dead.

☆   ☆   ☆

The seemingly interminable agony of Anglo-Irish relations drags on through the twentieth century, beset by misunderstandings, bitterness, resentment and suspicion and punctuated by recurring violence. A majority of people in Britain look westwards to the sister island with a sigh of weary despair. Ireland and its problems, many of them directly attributable to devious, foolish or even well-intentioned British Governments, can never have the same relevance to Britain as Britain has to the Irish. Sporadic bombing campaigns in British cities bring Ireland into the headlines and provoke an outraged response, but, by and large, relations with and within John Bull's other island are relegated to the tail-end of the priority list in the forlorn hope that least said, soonest mended.

Erskine Childers senior was one Englishman who became totally absorbed by the search for a solution to the age-old question and finally despaired of British intentions. His involvement in Ireland ended in tragedy and his name was widely reviled as that of a man who turned his back on his country to foment trouble in another. Mourned only by his family and a small circle of latter-day political associates, he was laid to rest in a simple ceremony at the Republican Plot in Glasnevin Cemetery, Dublin and allowed no proper funeral.

Fifty-two years later the name Erskine Childers was synonymous with peace and reconciliation as Ireland responded to the loss of a beloved Head of State with a spontaneous outpouring of grief and affectionate sympathy. The President's funeral in St Patrick's Cathedral, Dublin attracted the largest gathering of crowned heads and rulers ever to assemble on Irish soil and included the British Prime Minister and Leader of the Opposition. There was no room even for the R.T.E. Symphony Orchestra who especially asked to play at the Funeral Service as a tribute to the man largely responsible for forming the Orchestra and ever devoted to its welfare and to promoting music generally.*

Such unusually contrasting obsequies are really the key to a single story, as it is impossible to separate the parallels and opposites of this father and son who both wore themselves out serving Ireland. Born in London and educated at English public schools and Trinity College, Cambridge, they outwardly always remained cast in that mould. Erskine senior was orphaned at the age of thirteen and made his own way prompted largely by his experiences and a philosophy which continually evolved. But his son's life was inspired and dominated by his father's ideals and a death-cell promise given in adolescence, from which he never wavered.

From the time that he moved to Ireland the younger Erskine, though his background was totally different to that of his colleagues, found his outlook and philosophy blending easily with men and women of the generation which came into politics for an ideal and dedicated itself to building up both a party and a State. Personal comfort and prosperity took second place to duty and service, and the last words he spoke were warning his countrymen of a threat to future health and happiness.

Erskine Childers's political career touched a variety of spheres to all of which he brought a depth of vision, sense of purpose, energy and enthusiasm. An ability to grasp the essentials of a political or economic issue combined with a certain detachment, enabling seemingly intractable issues to be analysed without bias or prejudice. A conscientious and methodical administrator, he had an eye for detail and

*The Orchestra paid its tribute at the first Memorial Service in November 1975.

inherited great powers of concentration from his father and grandfather. A mild, courteous manner and kindly demeanour disguised a purposeful inner toughness.

Dedicated to Ireland and her welfare he nevertheless scorned a nationalism that was narrow and negative in thought and expression, and totally rejected violence. Reconciliation rather than recrimination was his by-word. An outside perspective laced his thinking and an inter-national dimension coloured his approach. As the first Irish European in public life he retained a warm affection for his native land. In looking to the future rather than dwelling in the past he sometimes appeared a man before his time, yet few in 1984 would scoff at his oft-repeated warnings on such subjects as dangers to the environment, drug-taking among young people, the stress factor in modern life and the need to plan for an increase in leisure time.

Although he was respected and well liked as a politician, it was only as First Citizen that Erskine Childers was able to give himself fully to the people. Though a prisoner of protocol he succeeded in taking the Presidency among them and injecting life and vigour into what had seemed hitherto a remote and almost irrelevant office. Though his speeches and pronouncements were more limited than he originally envisaged, Irish society was made aware that there was a relevant and meaningful role for the Head of State.

In stimulating an awareness of long-term needs and aspirations, individuals and local voluntary community efforts were encouraged to believe that they had an important role to play in shaping the destiny of the nation. The ordinary citizen quickly came to regard President Erskine Childers as a friend and he made a positive impact, though his style lost nothing in dignity or nobility. Warm affection and a sense of personal grief was reflected in the faces of people filing past the coffin of the President when his body lay in state in St Patrick's Hall in Dublin, or lining the route of the funeral procession from the city to the

Wicklow Hills, where Erskine Childers was laid to rest in the quiet hillside churchyard at Derralossary, above the village of Roundwood.

Both the Erskine Childerses were continually taunted as 'English' in a pejorative sense, and though this was undoubtedly a factor in sealing the fate of the elder man, it proved no handicap to the younger, whose Cambridge accent may even have provided an unexpected bonus in the race for the Presidency. Much of the credit for this must lie with Erskine Childers himself, for his integrity, devotion to reconciliation, loyalty to his party and sheer hard work won the hearts of the Irish people. Through this supreme example his father's own life has been re-examined and judgements made at a time of great emotional stress have been revised.

In 1922 it was widely held that the elder Erskine had squandered his life needlessly on a doomed cause, yet who, sixty years later, could echo this in the light of his elder son's dedicated career? Andrew Boyle wrote that the father's greatness was marred by 'an ungovernable tendency to stand in his own light',[11] yet his son consciously lived in his shadow and found strength and fulfilment by following the path marked out by a condemned father and clearly signposted by a devoted widow and mother. His life shines out in stark contrast to the anguish and horror that has overshadowed Anglo-Irish relations in recent times.

SOURCE REFERENCES

Chapter I. A London Childhood

1 Letter dated 7 April 1905.
2 Letter from HMS *Engadine* dated 11 October 1914.
3 Childers correspondence.
4 *Ibid.*
5 *Ibid.*
6 *Ibid.*
7 Letter from Erskine Childers senior to Robert Barton dated 23 May 1916.
8 Andrew Boyle: *The Riddle of Erskine Childers* p. 186.
9 As 7 above.
10 Childers correspondence.

Chapter II. Ireland and Tragedy

1 Childers papers.
2 Childers correspondence.
3 *Ibid.*
4 Letter dated 9 July 1918.
5 Letter from Erskine Childers senior to J. J. Horgan of Cork dated 26 September 1918.
6 Childers correspondence.
7 The Rev. Humphrey Whistler's notes to author.
8 Report of Treaty Debates.
9 *Dáil Reports,* Vol. 1 p. 859.
10 Testimony of Erskine Childers to Andrew Boyle.
11 Hilary Pyle: *Jack B. Yeats* p. 119.

Chapter III. Reverberations and Romance

1 Testimony of school contemporaries.
2 *Glasgow Herald,* 24 November 1922.
3 Notes from the Hon. Mervyn Roberts to author.
4 Notes from the Hon. Mervyn Roberts and the Rev. Humphrey Whistler to author.
5 Humphrey Carpenter: *W. H. Auden — A Biography* p. 28.

Chapter IV. An Unusual Undergraduate

1 Childers papers.
2 *The Old Vicarage, Grantchester.* Written by Rupert Brooke in 1912.
3 *Boston Globe*, 20 June 1925.
4 Notes from the Hon. Mervyn Roberts to author.
5 Notes from Mrs Winslow Eddy to author.

Chapter V. A Parisian Interlude

1 *Dáil Reports*, Vol. 247 col. 1690.
2 Wellesley College Magazine 1930.

Chapter VI. In the Shadow of the Riddle

1 *Dáil Reports*, Vol. 1 p. 2405.
2 *New Yorker*, January 1975.
3 *The Times*, 23 December 1932.
4 Notes from Mr C. E. F. Trench to author.
5 *The Irish Times*, 19 May 1976.
6 Notes from a lecture given to Dublin Rotary Club on 21 October 1963 by C. Gordon Lambert.
7 Gerald Boland's Story: *The Irish Times*, 11 October 1968.
8 *Longford Leader*, 11 June 1938.

Chapter VII. Ascending the Fianna Fáil Ladder

1 *Westmeath Independent*, 4 March 1939.
2 *Dáil Reports*, Vol. 72 col. 380.
3 Terence de Vere White: *Ireland* p. 9.
4 *Longford Leader*, 6 April 1941.
5 Notes from Mr Erskine B. Childers to author.
6 *Dáil Reports*, Vol. 83 col. 478 et seq.
7 Private paper dated 31 August 1942.
8 *Longford Leader*, 3 April 1943.
9 *The Irish Times*, 7 December 1944.
10 *Evening Herald*, 9 May 1945.
11 *The Irish Press*, 5 November 1945.
12 *Dáil Reports*, Vol. 117 col. 1029 et seq.
13 Childers papers.

Chapter VIII. Government under 'The Chief'

1 *Dáil Reports*, Vol. 126 col.1487 et seq.

2 *Ibid.*
3 *The Irish Press,* 14 July 1951.
4 *The Irish Times,* 16 June 1951.
5 *Longford News,* 19 January 1952.
6 Childers Papers.
7 *Dáil Reports,* Vol. 134 col. 917 et seq.
8 *The Irish Times,* 28 October 1952.
9 Memo. to Secretary dated 27 May 1954.
10 *Dáil Reports,* Vol. 146 col. 358.
11 *Longford Leader,* 13 April 1957.
12 *Dáil Reports,* Vol. 171 col. 1642.

Chapter IX. One of the Lemass Invincibles

1 *The Irish Press,* 12 May 1971.
2 *Sunday Independent,* 25 October 1959.
3 Erskine Childers's speech to Dublin Central Council of Fianna Fáil on 25 April 1961.
4 *Dáil Reports,* Vol. 182 cols. 999 to 1003.
5 Jack White: *Minority Report,* Chapter 9.
6 Testimony of Dr Thekla Beere to author.
7 *The Irish Times,* 24 August 1961.
8 *Cork Examiner,* 17 October 1961.

Chapter X. Health — and Horror in the North

1 *The Irish Times,* 14 August 1969.
2 *Ibid.*
3 Kevin Boland: *Up Dev!* p. 11 et seq.
4 *Magill,* June 1980.
5 *Dáil Reports,* Vol. 244 col. 1767.
6 *Dáil Reports,* Vol. 259 col. 1585.
7 *The Irish Independent,* Vol. 246 col. 1326 et seq.
8 *Dáil Reports,* Vol. 246 col. 1326 et seq.
9 *Ibid.*
10 Letter dated 11 December 1972.
11 *Dáil Reports,* Vol. 247 col. 1644.
12 *Dáil Reports,* Vol. 247 cols. 1689 to 1694.
13 *Dáil Reports,* Vol. 256 cols. 1498 to 1500.
14 *Dáil Reports,* Vol. 255 col. 2540.
15 *The Sunday Press,* 3 July 1983. Interview with Frank Aiken junior.
16 *The Irish Press,* 9 January 1972.

17 *The Sunday Press*, 10 October 1971.
18 *The Irish Times*, 6 May 1971.
19 *The Irish Times*, 28 July 1971.
20 *The Irish Times*, 14 August 1972.

Chapter XI. A Reluctant Candidate

1 *The Irish Press*, 21 February 1973.
2 *The Irish Times*, 26 February 1973.
3 Testimony of Mr Jack Lynch to author.
4 *Clare Champion*, 11 May 1973.
5 *Munster Express*, 4 May 1973.
6 *The Irish Times*, 21 May 1973.
7 *The Irish Times*, 24 May 1973.
8 *Irish Independent*, 1 June 1973.
9 *The Irish Times*, 1 June 1973.
10 *The Irish Press*, 1 June 1973.

Chapter XII. A President for All the Nation

1 The Earl of Longford and T. P. O'Neill: *Eamon de Valera* p. 455.
2 Michael McDunphy: *The President of Ireland — His Powers, Functions and Duties* p. 5.
3 Thomas Davis Lecture: 'The Presidency in Historical Perspective'. Broadcast on 20 May 1973.
4 *Longford Leader*, 3 June 1945.
5 *The Irish Times*, 21 January 1974.
6 *The Irish Times*, 22 June 1976. Interview with Chris O'Sullivan.
7 *Radio Times*, 8–15 December 1973.
8 *The Irish Times*, 7 April 1974.
9 *Life and Environment* (An Taisce Journal), October 1974.
10 *The Irish Times*, 20 May 1974. 'European Diary' by Fergus Pyle.
11 Andrew Boyle: *The Riddle of Erskine Childers* p. 326.

BIBLIOGRAPHY

Kevin Boland: *Up Dev!* (Published privately, Dublin 1977).

Andrew Boyle: *The Riddle of Erskine Childers* (Hutchinson, London 1977).

Humphrey Carpenter: *W. H. Auden — A Biography* (Geo. Allen & Unwin, London 1981).

Joseph Carroll: *Ireland in the War Years 1939—45* (David & Charles, Newton Abbot 1975).

Tim Pat Coogan: *Ireland since the Rising* (Pall Mall Press, London, 1966).

Michael Cunningham: *Monaghan, County of Intrigue* (Published privately, Donegal 1979).

The Earl of Longford: *Peace by Ordeal* (Jonathan Cape, London 1935).

The Earl of Longford and T .P. O'Neill: *Eamon de Valera* (Hutchinson, London 1970).

Michael McDunphy: *The President of Ireland — His Powers, Functions and Duties* (Browne & Nolan, Dublin 1945).

Francis MacManus and others: *The Years of the Great Test* (Mercier Press, Cork 1967).

Hilary Pyle: *Jack B. Yeats* (Routledge & Kegan Paul, London 1970).

Terence de Vere White: *Ireland* (Thames & Hudson, London 1968).

The Anglo-Irish (Gollancz, London 1972).

Kevin O'Higgins (Methuen, London 1948).

Jack White: *Minority Report* (Gill & Macmillan, Dublin 1975).

Burke Wilkinson: *The Zeal of the Convert* (Colin Smythe, Gerrards Cross 1977).

211

Basil Williams: *Erskine Childers. A Sketch based on Memories and Letters* (Published privately, London 1925).

Reports of Dáil Debates   *Hibernia*   *Magill*   *New Yorker*

Clare Champion	*Irish Independent*	*Sunday Independent*
Cork Examiner	*Longford Leader*	*Sunday Press*
Daily Telegraph	*Longford News*	*The Irish Press*
Evening Herald	*Munster Express*	*The Irish Times*
Evening Press	*Northern Standard*	*The Times*
		Westmeath Independent

INDEX

Note. The abbreviation EHC has been used throughout for Erskine H. Childers. Numbers in italics refer to illustrations.

213

Index

wife's death, 104
second marriage, 113-4

Career
In travel business, 59, 61-4, 65,
66-7
on *Irish Press* staff, 70, 74, 78, 81
early political career, 89-105
at Blackwood Hodge, 101, 108
at Pye Telecommunications,
116-7
Minister for Posts and
Telegraphs, ix, 106-10, 114-6,
138
Minister for Lands, Forests and
Fisheries, 118-9
Minister of Transport and Power,
ix, 123-40
Minister for Health, ix, 141,
145-7, 152, 161-2, 165, 166-7,
168
Deputy Prime Minister
(Tánaiste), xii, 141, 147, 152-4,
163-4, 178
Vice-President of Fianna Fáil, 149
Presidential campaign, 166,
160-70, 171-83
Inauguration, 180-3
as President, 184-203
assessment of career, 204-6
death and funeral, 203, 204,
205-6
characteristics
foresight, 24
reserve/diffidence, 137-8, 149
honours and doctorate, 119,
171, 199

letters quoted:
to sister, 12, 20
to father, 28, 29
to mother, 29, 35, 60
to de Valera, 39
to Ruth C, 41, 44, 46-7, 48-9,
50, 51, 54, 55, 61, 62, 67,
70-1, 76; not quoted, 65, 70

recreations:
cycling and fitness, 78-9, 95,
117
gardening, 201, 202

music, 9, 24, 115
poetry, 52
religious beliefs, 15, 37-8, 117,
170, 175
relationships:
with children and young
people, 197-8
with Lemass, 135-6
with Rita C, 117
with Ruth C, 37, 52, 104
with staff, 129
wives, *see* Childers: Rita; Ruth
children, *see* Childers: Caitlinn;
Erskine Barton; Margaret;
Nessa;
Roderick Winthrop; Ruth Ellen
Childers, Hugh Culling Eardley, 2,
164, 192
Childers, John, M.P., 2
Childers, Colonel John Walbanke, 2
Childers, Margaret (daughter), 83,
103, 104, 111
Childers, Molly (mother), 1, 4-5, 7,
12, 16, 20, 25, 77, 114
wedding, 5
early married life, 5-6, 8-9
political activities, 11, 23, 37, 39,
47, 66, 69
war work, 12-13
reluctance to move to Ireland, 22
and husband's execution, 32
and controversy over son's
marriage, 54, 56
visits EHC in Paris, 66
disposes of *Asgard*, 74
urges EHC to learn Irish, 93
death, 132
letters to EHC, quoted, 11, 13,
14-15, 19-20, 27-8, 31, 34,
57-8, 60-1, 68-9, 88
EHC letters to, quoted, 29, 31, 35
correspondence with Ruth Dow
(later Mrs Erskine H. Childers), 36
relationship with husband, 104
vision of EHC outside politics, 69,
183
Childers, Nessa (daughter), 117, 132,
172, 177, 189, 197, 202
Childers, Rita (second wife), xii, 118,
132, 136, 150, 202

215

Index

Index